GLOBAL PERSPECTIVES ON
QUALITY IN HIGHER EDUCATION

Global Perspectives on Quality in Higher Education

Edited by
DAVID DUNKERLEY AND WAI SUM WONG

LONDON AND NEW YORK

First published 2001 by Ashgate Publishing

Reissued 2018 by Routledge
2 Park Square, Milton Park, Abingdon, Oxon OX14 4RN
711 Third Avenue, New York, NY 10017, USA

Routledge is an imprint of the Taylor & Francis Group, an informa business

Copyright © The contributors 2001

All rights reserved. No part of this book may be reprinted or reproduced or utilised in any form or by any electronic, mechanical, or other means, now known or hereafter invented, including photocopying and recording, or in any information storage or retrieval system, without permission in writing from the publishers.

Notice:
Product or corporate names may be trademarks or registered trademarks, and are used only for identification and explanation without intent to infringe.

Publisher's Note
The publisher has gone to great lengths to ensure the quality of this reprint but points out that some imperfections in the original copies may be apparent.

Disclaimer
The publisher has made every effort to trace copyright holders and welcomes correspondence from those they have been unable to contact.

A Library of Congress record exists under LC control number: 2001094262

ISBN 13: 978-1-138-70194-6 (hbk)
ISBN 13: 978-0-415-79374-2 (pbk)
ISBN 13: 978-1-315-20989-0 (ebk)

Contents

List of Figure and Tables	vii
Preface	viii
Foreword	x

1. Introduction — 1
   David Dunkerley and Wai Sum Wong

2. The Quality Assurance of Higher Education in Hong Kong — 11
   John C.Y. Leong and Wai Sum Wong

3. Quality Assurance and Evaluation of Higher Education in Mainland China — 34
   Xu Demin, Qi Suiyuan and Wang Runxiao

4. Towards a European Dimension — 46
   Marie-Odile Ottenwaelter

5. Academic Review in the United Kingdom — 57
   John Randall

6. Quality Assurance of Higher Education in Denmark — 70
   Christian Thune

7. Accreditation and Quality in the United States: Practice and Pressures — 91
   Judith S. Eaton

8. Chile: Quality Assurance in a Context of Change — 106
   María José Lemaitre

9. Strengthening Quality Assurance in Australian Higher Education — 123
   Kwong Lee Dow

10. External Quality Assurance in Higher Education in South Africa — 143
    Danie Jacobs

List of Contributors 155

Index 158

List of Figure and Tables

Table 2.1	Student enrolment (fte) of UGC-funded programmes 1998–1999	12
Table 2.2	A summary of institutional reviews and course validations conducted by the HKCAA at Hong Kong education institutions	17
Table 8.1	Growth of institutions and enrolment in higher education institutions, 1980–2000	108
Table 8.2	Results of actions taken by the Consejo Superior de Educacion, 1990–2000	113
Figure 8.1	Elements of a quality assurance scheme	119

Preface

John C.Y. Leong
Chairman, Hong Kong Council for Academic Accreditation

This book on quality in higher education around the world is published as a commemorative issue on the occasion of the tenth anniversary of the Hong Kong Council for Academic Accreditation (HKCAA). At the time the HKCAA was established as a statutory body in 1990, to oversee the quality of the expanding higher education sector in Hong Kong, it was a forefront development not only in Hong Kong but also in the Asia Pacific Region. The quality assurance movement in higher education, although well developed in some countries at that time, was still at an embryonic stage in many parts of the world. The HKCAA foresaw the need for global cooperation in this strategic development and took the lead to establish the International Network for Quality Assurance Agencies in Higher Education, which has grown to be the only international organisation for accreditation and quality assurance organisations and which has remained at the centre stage of this world movement to promote and safeguard the quality of education.

Hong Kong has itself, in the meantime, risen to the challenge of many new developments including the expansion of post-secondary education, the globalisation of education and the emergence of distance education, and the influx of foreign qualifications into the labour market. All of these have required new and innovative forms of quality assurance in order to safeguard the quality of the education system and the workforce. All these have brought about a transfiguration in the role of the external quality assurance body, the HKCAA. At the same time they have posed new questions regarding the relationship of the external quality assurance body; with the rest of society which has come to demand far more information and greater consumer protection; with the higher education sector which has become more mature and diversified; and with the Government which has increasingly adopted a greater regulatory role. It is undoubted that similar phenomena mark the quality assurance scene in other parts of the world. What is needed is therefore a sharing of issues and problems and a sharing of vision. Hence the HKCAA has pooled the experience of quality assurance experts from around the world, some of whom are currently or formerly members of the Council, to contribute their thoughts in this publication which hopefully will depict not only the multifaceted landscape of quality assurance in the selected countries but also shed light on the common ground and common strategies in the way ahead.

Foreword

Fanny Law
Secretary for Education and Manpower
Hong Kong Special Administrative Region, China

How to assure quality in higher education in an expanding, but increasingly competitive and cost-conscious global market, operating under disparate circumstances, including the unregulated realm of cyberspace, is one of the major challenges facing universities and governments worldwide.

In Hong Kong, we have recently set ourselves new goals for further expanding our post-secondary and higher education system, while at the same time encouraging greater diversity of provision, containing costs and maintaining standards. We also aim to facilitate progression, articulation, portability and recognition of qualifications between a broader range of providers, across sectors and among levels.

In order to achieve these ambitious goals, our quality assurance system must have credibility, inspire confidence and maintain recognition among employers and professional bodies.

We have developed, with the support of the University Grants Committee and the Hong Kong Council for Academic Accreditation, a system that is institution-based, but has external and international input; is robust, without being intrusive; and is responsive and flexible, without compromising on standards.

This system has been developed drawing on experience and expertise from around the world and it also enshrines the principle of continuous quality improvement. We are therefore constantly looking for ways to develop and improve it further to cope with present and future challenges.

The publication of this volume providing a cross-country perspective and comparative studies on the issues of quality assurance in higher education is therefore timely for us and, I suspect, for many others. I am personally convinced of the efficacy of this kind of international sharing of experience and therefore welcome the Hong Kong Council for Academic Accreditation's initiative to produce this book.

I also congratulate the editors for drawing together the various strands of international experience.

This book serves as an excellent way to mark the tenth anniversary of the Hong Kong Council for Academic Accreditation, which has, for the past decade, been providing the government and higher education institutions in Hong Kong with professional and internationally informed advice on quality assurance issues.

Chapter One

Introduction

David Dunkerley and Wai Sum Wong

The title of this book, *Global Perspectives on Quality in Higher Education*, contains within it two of the most widely used words in contemporary academic and lay discourse – 'global' and 'quality'. Twenty years ago neither word would have figured much in any text; today the literature is replete with both of them. It is therefore necessary, in the first instance, to discuss what the words mean and whether there is any link between them. 'Global', 'globalisation', 'globalism', 'globality' all describe different phenomena and/ or processes but consistently point to a changed and changing relationship between 'the global' and 'the local'. Giddens (1990, p. 64), for example, defines globalisation as 'the intensification of worldwide social relationships which link distant places in such a way that local happenings are shaped by events occurring many miles away and *vice-versa*.' Similarly, Spybey (1996, p. 5) notes that the influence of globalisation operates not just on the large scale but also penetrates 'the significant, the routine and the most intimate aspects of life.' At the same time it might be argued that 'the global' is a kind of phenomenological aspect of the local meeting the global in the sense of a growing awareness in people's minds everywhere of the world conceived as a loose entity rather than as a unified whole.

There is certainly a 'coming together' but equally there is a simultaneous fragmentation. The most obvious examples of the former lie in a form of global culture generated by the Western media (especially via satellite transmissions), by global icons (e.g. Madonna, Michael Jackson or Vanessa Mae) and the global proliferation of products and Western consumer goods (McDonalds, Coca-Cola, Levi-Strauss). However, fragmentation is visible. Examples might include the threatened disintegration of 'the nation' whether it be Spain and the Basque Separatists, Sri Lanka and the Tamil Tigers, Canada and the Quebecois or the growth of separatist nationalism in Wales and Scotland in the UK.

While examples of the global impacting on the local are legion through the existence of global cultural and cultural products, the local can also be swept up into the global. Thus local products are marketed globally as conveying a form of national 'essence'. Thus Fosters lager is seen as 'essentially Australian', malt whisky as 'essentially Scottish', the ubiquitous Irish bar as 'essentially Irish'. Similarly, local foods have been globalised – Italian pizza, Indian curry, Cantonese cuisine. Notions of 'difference' and of 'foreign-ness' can win competitive advantage in the fashion industry as global companies such as Benetton use Indian, African and Oriental styles for the next 'seasonal look'.

It is undeniable that in many senses the world is shrinking and that 'McDonaldisation' (Ritzer, 1996) and 'Coca-colonisation' is a form of 'recolonisation of the non-Western world by fetishised Western goods carrying with them hugely invasive connotations of Western success and affluence ... this process is extremely difficult to arrest' (Beynon and Dunkerley, 2000, p. 23).

A question central to this book, then, is whether these wider arguments concerning the globalising process can be applied to the other key word in the book's title – quality. Is it now possible to think of the McDonaldisation of quality assurance in higher education? Have Western models been imposed on local situations creating a kind of borderless and seamless world of quality assurance subject to a form of twenty-first century imperialist hegemony? Before that question can be addressed, it is necessary first to explore what is meant by 'quality' in higher education.

As with the term 'global' and its associates, 'quality' has become one of the watchwords of the early twenty-first century, coming into popular vogue and usage about 20 years ago. 'Quality of life', 'quality circles', 'total quality management', 'quality products', 'quality service' – the prefix 'quality' has entered the lexicon of everyday life. And nowhere is this more prevalent than in higher education where agencies, managers and committees are now all dedicated to and employ the word 'quality'.

It is perhaps over the last 15 years that higher education has embraced quality and quality assurance on a scale not hitherto seen. This is not to say that there had not previously been concerns with quality – far from it. Universities have always played an important gate-keeping role for the traditional professions such as law, engineering and medicine and the assessment of the quality of entrants and graduates in order to meet the minimum professional thresholds has always been part of their role. Similarly, universities have been concerned to ensure the quality of their staff both on appointment and whilst in post. The PhD has for the best part of a century been seen as the hallmark of an academic's quality and provides his/her fitness for appointment. The quality of the academic's written output has long since been assured through the peer review system operated by journals and the grant awarding bodies.

What started in the 1980s and is continuing today is something rather different in both form and rationale. Quality and quality assurance issues in higher education rose to prominence both nationally and internationally. In that relatively short period the concern with quality and quality assurance has risen towards the top of the higher education agenda. This concern is articulated by university managers themselves, by external agencies deliberately established to assess and reward quality and, increasingly, by the 'clients' of higher education – the students, the employers and, importantly, the state. The days of assuming that a graduate could turn his/her hand to anything because of the demonstrable intellectual/analytical powers bestowed by a university education have passed. Instead, the position is moving to one where employer and work-based needs directly influence the curriculum in many disciplines.

This rise to prominence has not come about by the universities being swept along on the quality tide so obvious among economic producers and service providers. Public and government concerns about standards have certainly come to the fore. The chronology of these concerns and the move away from an elitist to a mass higher education system in many countries is not simply coincidence. The battle-cry of the New Right in the 1980s of 'More means worse!' can still be heard. Coupled with a declining unit of resource universities, their paymasters were forced to respond in order to allay and reassure the public, the employers and the politicians that more might mean different but that more still met a measurable and acceptable quality threshold.

The last decades of the twentieth century also witnessed a much greater mobility of labour internationally, especially of professionally-trained labour. This trend continues. Within the European Union, for example, the Schengen Agreement of 1985 incorporated into the 1997 Treaty of Amsterdam allows, *inter alia*, for the free movement of persons throughout the EU. Newly trained social workers and nurses from Australia have become essential workers in many London social care agencies and hospitals as young people use their internationally recognised qualifications to help them in their European 'gap year'. The flight of many British academics (the 'brain drain') to North America and the antipodes continues and is facilitated by an acceptance of the quality of their qualifications and their research outputs.

A further reason for quality's rise to prominence is also undoubtedly the rise of what has been referred to as the 'Evaluative State'. Henkel (1998, p. 285) points out that 'Evaluation and evaluation studies developed substantially in the US in a period of optimism and expansion ... They were associated with modernisation, the rationalisation of society and the policy process and with the growth and improvement of the public sector.' As noted evaluation of higher education and of academics is nothing new but has traditionally been underpinned by a kind of liberalism described by J.S. Mill where individualism and integrity were paramount. Arguably, this position has shifted as the external demands for assurance have increased and as these become part of a political process. As Henkel points out the rise of the Evaluative State has brought with it many issues and that they 'reflect how the dominance of academics is being challenged by a range of stakeholders in higher education evaluation and how questions are being raised about what different forms of knowledge might be required in such evaluation. They force those concerned with higher education to review for themselves some of the basic conceptual and epistemological issues of evaluative theory and practice...' (1998, p. 294). Without doubt this involves a more critical analysis of values as well as an analysis of power and power relationships within universities and between them and the state.

Coming back to the earlier central question of the link between the global and higher education quality, Brennan and Shah (2000, p. 1) use Teichler's analogy of

> the growth of a world religion, a religion whose believers are divided into many different sects and who confront non-believers daily in their working lives. The sects tend to be evangelical, seeking to spread their views of the world to others and, like religions, frequently enter into uneasy alliances with secular powers ... to achieve their ends. In many cases it may be suspected that it is the secular power which is using the religion to pursue *its* ends.

Although they themselves do not sign up wholeheartedly to the analogy it remains a useful one. The role of external forces cannot be underestimated, whether they are external to the institution or external to a particular country. Some of these forces are global as already suggested while others arise from the imposition of practices derived from 'new public management' involving accountability, assuring value for money and providing confidence to a more questioning and cynical public.

The chapters in this volume directly or indirectly address these issues by looking at various aspects of quality, quality assurance and quality maintenance in a range of countries. Some countries have been at the forefront of the 'quality movement' – arguably Brennan and Shah's evangelists on a mission. Others are only just now working through what system of quality evaluation should be employed. The question remains whether it is possible to identify global patterns or whether the local conditions and interests prevail.

Hong Kong provides a useful starting point in answering this question since before 1997 it was a British colony and subject to British ideas and interventions. Thus, the early assessments of courses and of non-university higher education institutions was carried out by the erstwhile British Council for National Academic Awards. As Leong and Wong point out in Chapter Two the Ordinance establishing the Hong Kong Council for Academic Accreditation (HKCAA) based the Council firmly within the British tradition. Furthermore, the assessment of research undertaken periodically by the Hong Kong Universities Grants Committee has been an almost exact replication of the British Research Assessment Exercises. All of this is unsurprising given the political position of Hong Kong until the 1997 hand-over to China. What is distinctive about the system extant in contemporary Hong Kong is the very cosmopolitan nature of quality assurance exercises involving, as they do, extensive use of overseas advisors and experts. This is not a reflection of a lack of local talent or a lack of confidence; far from it. It reflects a genuine desire to use what is best and most appropriate both regionally and internationally. The Government of the Special Administrative Region is now starting to unfold its bold plan to raise the participation rate of senior secondary school leavers in higher education to 60 per cent by 2011.

The sheer size of higher education provision in China is highlighted in Xu's chapter both in terms of the number of higher education institutions and the actual number of students. The highly centralised system is also worthy of note given that the Chinese Higher Education Law has established government norms relating to teaching quality in the PRC. These norms relate to every university department and every university teacher. Although there are internal quality assurance systems, governmental controls remain paramount. The position might be changing slowly as the move to a market economy takes place thus suggesting that employers might begin to have more say over what takes place in the universities. Nevertheless, the position that has developed over the last 20 years is clearly one where the influence of the state has been paramount. However, one also observes that this drive for quality assurance as spearheaded by the state is paralleled by a growth of awareness and participation in quality assurance among academics and administrators in the institutions; an emergence of semi-independent accreditation bodies which work for the state; and a proliferation of discussion and theorising on topics of quality assurance among academics, as well as non-governmental bodies with an interest in the quality assurance of education. All these point to the emergence of a diversity of stakeholders in matters of quality assurance, a scene which might become not too different from the western countries in future.

Turning to Europe, Ottenwaelter demonstrates in Chapter Four how within the European Union and its candidate countries there has been a clear move in recent years towards harmonisation of both systems and practices especially in the area of quality assurance. This, of course, is part of the EU's drive towards a European identity that is over and beyond individual national identities. She points out that the increase in size (student numbers, universities themselves and expenditure) has been the primary motivator for the introduction of evaluation procedures. The various European initiatives described by Ottenwaelter all point to the desire for a European dimension that will promote mobility and employability across national boundaries. The 1999 Bologna Declaration might, in time, prove to be a decisive turning point in realising this European dimension especially if compatible quality assurance systems can be developed throughout Europe as well as the development of European quality labels based on independent evaluation. Although many questions as to the likely shape and direction of European harmonisation remain unanswered the direction in which quality assurance is moving may act as a model for other multi-country groupings in, for example, South America, South-East Asia and Southern Africa.

Randall's argument in Chapter Five is similar to the one used above – that the move to a mass participation system of higher education has been a global one and that in most countries there have been increasing calls for universities to demonstrate the maintenance and enhancement of standards. Furthermore, he argues, many countries now have national quality evaluation bodies of one kind or another. The Quality Assurance Agency for Higher Education in the UK has, in many ways, led the way for other countries in its relatively short life. Examples might include the subject level reviews, bench-marking and the development of a Qualifications Framework. The new method of quality assurance – the academic review – is being used for the first time in Scotland this year and will extend to the rest of the UK in the academic year 2001–02. The chapter explains in some detail what the academic review method involves and, in particular, shows how quality may be assured through reporting on programme outcome standards, the quality of learning opportunities and the institutional management of standards and quality.

Although Denmark, as Thune points out in Chapter Six, has only introduced a formalised system for quality assurance relatively recently, it is clear that although distinctive it has been greatly influenced by developments in other countries. Indeed, as elsewhere, the enlargement of higher education provision provided a major spur to the introduction of a quality assurance framework. It is interesting to note that the higher education participation rate in Denmark is already 56 per cent and that around 40 per cent of a year group finishes with a degree. Although a country with a population of only 5 million, Denmark has a remarkably complex yet extensive system of higher education provision. The relatively new Danish Evaluation Institute (EVA) uses a quality assurance methodology that is not unfamiliar to other European countries. It has not, however, been involved in accreditation in the sense of arriving at a clear yes/no answer as to whether quality meets articulated standards. The international trend towards accreditation in this sense is one that Denmark and other Scandinavian countries will soon have to address. Interestingly, Denmark has clearly been anxious to participate in and learn from international initiatives and developments. Indeed, EVA has played a major role in bringing about the kind of European cooperation outlined by Ottenwaelter in Chapter Four.

Although the highly centralised system of China with its large population has been noted above, the United States represents a large country both in terms of population and geographical area but where decentralisation of accreditation is a key feature. The immensity of the US higher education system is demonstrated by the fact that it employs over half the population size of Denmark, has over 6,500 higher education institutions and has in excess of 20,000 accredited programmes. Although the term accreditation is used in the US its meaning is specific to that country. Thus, as Eaton shows in Chapter Seven an institution or programme is considered to be accredited if it meets the standards of an accrediting organisation, sustains means of assuring quality and maintain strategies for improving quality. Even when accredited status is acquired an institution or programme has then to gain the authority to operate by the individual state. The decentralised nature of the accreditation process can be seen in the respective work of the regional, national and specialised and professional agencies. The latter have themselves to go through periodic external review to maintain their recognised status; the review being undertaken either by the Council for Higher Education Accreditation (CHEA) or by the federal Department of Education. Eaton highlights a number of pressures currently being experienced by the accreditation process – these include the pressure for regional accreditors to operate nationally (in a sense this is a similar movement that has already been identified for European countries to operate more at the European level) and the pressure to increase international activity for precisely the kinds of reasons given above as education, graduates and academics become more globally mobile.

Chile provides a particularly interesting example of a country that has undergone a rapid shift from small-scale elite higher education to a mass participation model. In 1980 there were just eight higher education institutions with around 120,000 students; by 2000 there were 244 institutions attracting 417,000 students. A highly selective system has moved to one of relatively open access; the system is also characterised by a mixture of public and private institutions. Twenty years ago quality assurance systems were virtually nonexistent in Chile; the unregulated system allowed dozens of higher education institutions of dubious quality to open and to award degrees. This fascinating scenario is outlined by Lemaitre in Chapter Eight. She shows how at the national level the Chilean Higher Council for Education has developed into a very powerful body chaired, in fact, by the Minister of Education. Its powers include the forced closure of institutions and these powers have actually been used to close 17 institutions to date. Although voluntary, there is now a programme accreditation process undertaken by a National Commission for Accreditation. The incentive for undergoing the accreditation process is that funds may subsequently follow.

Lemaitre also outlines the likely workings of a South American regional accreditation body arising from MERCOSUR. Argentina, Brazil, Paraguay, Uruguay, Bolivia and Chile have come together in an attempt to harmonise their educational systems, to develop an integration process and to provide common training. It is early days but a memorandum of agreement has also been signed by all six participating countries to introduce a mechanism for the accreditation of degree programmes and the recognition of degrees.

The quality assurance system in Australia has had to take account of the federal political structure involving state, territory and Commonwealth governments. In Chapter Nine Lee Dow describes the very recent developments in higher education quality assurance in Australia and, in particular the set of regulatory protocols common to all levels of government as well as the establishment of a national audit body in 2000, the Australian Universities' Quality Agency (AUQA). Although historically Australia has adopted, with adjustment, many aspects British governance it is interesting to note that the AUQA has deliberately tried to avoid the expense and intrusiveness of the British system. Australia has moved to a mass system of higher education provided mainly by the public universities and a small number of private providers. The proportion of graduates in Australia has virtually doubled in the past decade. An unusual feature of Australian higher education is its attraction for overseas students – international students come from over 200 countries and it is estimated that around 117,000 overseas students will enrol in Australian universities by 2003. Up till now every university has had to undergo three consecutive years of audits and each university has to address quality issues with government. The new protocols will certainly strengthen an already strong system, as will the operations of the new AUQA.

A new national body for higher education quality assurance has also very recently been introduced in South Africa. In Chapter Ten Jacobs describes how post-apartheid South Africa has come to grips with widening access to higher education from the former position of a largely elite white student entry. Traditionally, the universities have dealt with quality matters themselves and only the technikon sector has had a central external quality assurance body (SERTEC). Some space is devoted to how SERTEC has operated and consideration is given to its successes and failures. The 1997 Higher Education Act established the Council on Higher Education with operational responsibility for higher education quality assurance. In order to discharge this responsibility an interim Higher Education Quality Committee (HEQC) has been established with far-reaching and new responsibilities for South African higher education. These include the promotion of quality assurance as well as the audit of mechanisms and the accreditation of programmes. For the first time, then, the whole of South African higher education will be subject to a consistent programme of quality assurance. Jacobs points out how the HEQC has deliberately considered systems of quality assurance extant in other countries and on the basis of its review has arrived at a structure combining self-evaluation and external peer review.

Although not comprehensively global, this volume has nevertheless taken examples of developments in quality assurance matters in higher education covering countries and regions that span the Americas, the southern hemisphere, Europe and Asia. The countries examined cover a wide variety of political ideologies, political histories of stability and recent rapid change, different stages of economic development and hugely different population sizes. On the face of it, a veritable heterogeneity with little in common. Yet it is surprising just how many similarities there actually are and it does come back to the question of whether a homogenising process is at work. Whether this is just another example of 'cultural imperialism' (Craft, 1994, p. ix) or a McDonaldisation of quality assurance is a moot point.

In all of the countries surveyed there has been a shift towards a mass participation system of higher education in recent times. In some cases the participation rate of the relevant age group is already high, in other cases clear targets have been set by government to achieve a high participation rate in a relatively short time. The growth in numbers of students and in the size of the higher education sector has raised concerns from several corners about the maintenance of standards especially where relations between government and higher education have been based primarily on self-regulation. Almost universally, it would appear, mechanisms have been introduced for the systematic and formalised assessment and review of quality in higher education and for ways of achieving improvement. These mechanisms invariably involve external scrutiny, some form of peer review and transparency coordinated by some national body. In some countries such a body is now well-established, in others the coordinating body has only just been established.

There is evidence of individual national systems cooperating in some kind of regional activity in order to promote harmonisation of quality assurance systems and hence portability of output in the sense of qualifications being recognised beyond national boundaries. The obvious examples are the developments in Europe and South America but other groupings are likely in the near future. For example, an Asia-Pacific grouping is already being discussed. It is also worth pointing out that the International Network of Quality Assurance Agencies in Higher Education currently has membership from over 50 countries from around the world – a truly global network.

Given that the pressures that higher education are under in most countries are similar (e.g. increasing student numbers, a declining unit of resource, the need to maintain standards) it is unremarkable to find that the reaction to these pressures are similar. The reaction and response is, in this sense, global. But in the same way that McDonalds makes local adjustments to what it offers (for example, in India, in Israel and in France) it remains a global corporation offering a very similar menu worldwide. The same would appear to be case with quality assurance in higher education – a global movement with local variation. This is not an all-conquering Westernisation nor a sinister form of cultural imperialism. Instead, it is a case of 'think globally, act locally'.

References

Beynon, J. and Dunkerley, D. (2000), *Globalisation: The Reader*, New York: Routledge.
Brennan, J. and Shah, T. (2000), *Managing Quality in Higher Education*, Buckingham: Open University Press.
Craft, A. (ed.) (1994), *International Developments in Assuring Quality in Higher Education*, London: Falmer.
Giddens, A. (1990), *The Consequences of Modernity*, Cambridge: Polity.
Henkel, M. (1998), 'Evaluation in Higher Education: Conceptual and epistemological foundations', *European Journal of Education*, 33, 3, pp. 285–97.
Ritzer, G. (1996), *The McDonaldization of Society: An investigation into the changing character of social life*, Thousand Oaks, Calif.: Pine Forge Press.
Spybey, T. (1996), *Globalisation and World Society*, Cambridge: Polity.

Chapter Two

The Quality Assurance of Higher Education in Hong Kong

John C.Y. Leong
The University of Hong Kong
and
Wai Sum Wong
Hong Kong Council for Academic Accreditation

Education in Hong Kong

The Education System

Tertiary education Education is an important issue in Hong Kong and one of the major items in public expenditure. In 2000, government expenditure on education was 23 per cent of its total budget and 4 per cent of Hong Kong's Gross Domestic Product, amounting to HK$45 billion. While primary and junior secondary education is compulsory and free, there is heavy subsidy for senior secondary and tertiary education. Public resources devoted to post-secondary education is 34.7 per cent of the budget on education. Education at the tertiary level is marked by keen competition for the available places. The government has expanded the tertiary sector to an extent such that degree-level education, by 1994/95, has been offered to about 18 per cent of the relevant age group compared to less than 9 per cent in 1989.

There are currently ten institutions offering degree programmes in Hong Kong, five of which, the Hong Kong Baptist University (HKBU), the Lingnan University (LU), The Chinese University of Hong Kong (CUHK), The Hong Kong University of Science and technology (HKUST) and The University of Hong Kong (HKU) offer undergraduate and postgraduate programmes. Three offer sub-degree, undergraduate and postgraduate programmes, namely, City University of Hong Kong (CityU), The Hong Kong Polytechnic University (PolyU) and The Open University of Hong Kong (OUHK). The Hong Kong Institute of Education (HKIEd), and The Hong Kong Academy for Performing Arts (APA) offer sub-degree and undergraduate programmes.

Entry to higher education is through the Hong Kong Advanced Level Examination (HKALE) which is a public examination taken after Secondary 7.

Degree-granting institutions offer three-year Bachelor degrees (except for some specialised degrees such as medicine and dentistry), taught Masters' degrees, Masters' degrees by research and doctoral degrees by research.

Degree-granting institutions are publicly funded in Hong Kong. The University Grants Committee is responsible for the allocation of funding to eight of the degree-granting institutions. The APA is funded through the Home Affairs Bureau, and the OUHK is self-financing. The government is considering allowing private institutions to become degree-awarding in the near future after proper accreditation.

Total student enrolment (full-time equivalent) at the eight UGC-funded institutions was 70,040 in 1998/99, including 45,523 undergraduate students, and about 9,000 postgraduate students (see Table 2.1).

Table 2.1 Student enrolment (fte) of UGC-funded programmes 1998–1999

Institution	Sub-degree	Under-graduate	Taught postgraduate	Research postgraduate	Total
CityU	5,103	7,412	1,090	356	13,961
HKBU	–	4,031	245	118	4,394
LU	–	2,119	–	16	2,135
CUHK	–	9,244	1,274	1,054	11,572
HKIEd	4,932	110	25	–	5,067
PolyU	4,813	7,760	890	333	13,796
HKUST	–	5,655	566	683	6,904
HKU	–	9,192	1,972	1,047	12,211
Total	14,848	45,523	6,062	3,607	70,040

Key

CityU	Hong Kong City University
HKBU	Hong Kong Baptist University
LU	Lingnan University
CUHK	Chinese University of Hong Hong
HKIEd	Hong Kong Institute of Education
PolyU	Hong Kong Polytechnic University
HKUST	Hong Kong University of Science and Technology
HKU	Hong Kong University

Source: Hong Kong 1999.

Post secondary college There is at present one college registered under the Post Secondary College Ordinance, the Hong Kong Shue Yan College. The College operates a four-year diploma programme. The Caritas Francis Hsu College, which offers four-year Higher Diplomas, is applying to be registered under the Ordinance.

Vocational education The Vocational Training Council provides publicly funded vocational and technical training courses, formerly at its technical colleges and technical institutes, which have been merged recently into a single institution, the Hong Kong Institute of Vocational Education. Courses offered include Diplomas, Higher Diplomas, Certificates, Higher Certificates and others, catering for Secondary 5 and Secondary 3 leavers.

Continuing education Apart from the OUHK which offers continuing education to those in employment at both the degree and sub-degree level, continuing education is provided by the continuing education departments/schools of the universities. These are mostly sub-degree level courses.

Primary and secondary education There are nine years of compulsory education starting from the age of six. Primary schooling provides six years of general education. Secondary education comprises junior secondary (secondary 1–3), senior secondary (4–5) and the sixth form (secondary 6–7).

There are three main types of secondary schools: grammar schools (providing 90 per cent of the places), technical schools and pre-vocational schools. These offer five-year secondary courses leading to the Hong Kong Certificate of Education Examination (HKCEE). A two-year sixth form course leads to the Hong Kong Advanced Level Examination (HKALE).

Administering the Education System

The Education and Manpower Bureau (EMB) The EMB formulates government policy for educational and labour issues, for consideration by the Executive Council.

The Education Commission The Education Commission is the government's highest advisory body on education. It is an independent body made up of educationalists, academics, and distinguished members of the community.

The University Grants Committee (UGC) The UGC advises the government on the application and allocation of funds, and the financial needs of designated higher education institutions. At present it administers public grants to eight of Hong Kong's tertiary institutions. It also advises government on specific aspects of development in higher education.

The Education Department The Director of Education, supported by the Education Department, is responsible for overseeing education at the kindergarten, primary and secondary levels. The Department is in control of all government schools.

The Hong Kong Council for Academic Accreditation (HKCAA) Established by Ordinance in 1990, the Hong Kong Council for Academic Accreditation is an independent statutory body with members appointed by the Chief Executive of Hong Kong, from the ranks of local academics, overseas academics, and local lay members of the community. The Council performs accreditation in respect of non-self-accrediting tertiary institutions and their programmes and provides advice to the government on educational standards and qualifications. Specifically the Council advises the Registrar of Non-local Courses on the registration of non-local courses conducted in Hong Kong under the Non-local Higher and Professional Education (Regulation) Ordinance. The Council also provides consultancy services in respect of the assessment of non-local qualifications for comparability to local standards; and is a source of information and advice to the government, the tertiary institutions, and the public on educational standards, accreditation, and the quality assurance of higher education.

Quality Assurance of Local Education: Establishment of External Quality Assurance Body

The Hong Kong Council for Academic Accreditation Ordinance

Hong Kong began to have its own system of external quality assurance in higher education starting with the establishment of the Hong Kong Council for Academic Accreditation in 1990 as a statutory body, to provide accreditation for higher education institutions in Hong Kong, and to provide authoritative advice to the Government of Hong Kong on matters of educational quality and quality assurance.

The government found there was a need to put in place external monitoring of the quality of higher education when there was a quick expansion of higher education in the 1980s, from a participation rate of 2 per cent for the 18–20 age group to a rate of 18 per cent. As existing institutions were upgraded to become degree awarding, the government found it necessary to engage, initially, an external body from the UK, the Council for National Academic Awards, to conduct reviews on these institutions and on their proposed degree programmes.

By 1987, the Government of Hong Kong considered it appropriate to develop a greater degree of self-sufficiency in the quality control of higher education, and hence desirable to set up Hong Kong's own system of academic accreditation. Plans were made to establish an independent statutory body for this purpose, starting with the setting up of the Provisional Hong Kong Council for Academic Accreditation in 1987. Eventually, the Hong Kong Council for Academic Accreditation Ordinance was enacted on 23 March 1990 and the statute commenced on 8 June 1990. The first chairman and members were also appointed on the same date.

The Binary Systems

Following the binary system in the UK, which segregates the higher education system into universities and non-universities, the work of the Hong Kong Council for Academic Accreditation was targeted at the non-university sector, which in the early 1990s comprised the Hong Kong Polytechnic, the City Polytechnic of Hong Kong, the Hong Kong Baptist College, the Lingnan College, the Hong Kong Academy for Performing Arts, and the Open Learning Institute of Hong Kong. These were newly upgraded or newly established degree-granting institutions that had not yet attained university status, but empowered by their respective ordinance to confer academic awards. Following the UK model, the old universities which were already in existence were not required to undergo external academic accreditation by the Hong Kong Council for Academic Accreditation.

In addition to the above, there were other tertiary institutions accredited over the years by the HKCAA, including the Hong Kong Institute of Education, the Hong Kong Shue Yan College, and the Caritas Francis Hsu College.

According to the HKCAA Ordinance, the HKCAA may perform academic accreditation on higher education institutions at the request of the University Grants Committee of Hong Kong; or at the direction of the Chief Executive; or at the request of the institution to be accredited together with the consent of the Chief Executive.

The Changing Scene of Academic Accreditation

It is one of the HKCAA's principles to promote the capability of the tertiary institutions to accredit its own degree programmes. In accordance with this a number of tertiary institutions have been judged to have reached a maturity stage where they can be responsible for their quality assurance and no longer required to be subject to external accreditation by the HKCAA. Thus the former Hong Kong Polytechnic, the City Polytechnic of Hong Kong, and Hong Kong Baptist College were granted self-accreditation status in 1993 by the UGC and subsequently renamed as universities. The Open Learning Institute of Hong Kong, after undergoing an institutional review conducted by the HKCAA, was granted self-accreditation status and was renamed the Open University of Hong Kong in 1996. The Lingnan College achieved the same status and became the Lingnan University in 1999.

Secondly, the target of accreditation has widened in recent years. The initial target of academic accreditation, as envisaged by the HKCAA Ordinance, was degree-level education. Thus the work of HKCAA was limited to degree-awarding institutions and their degree programmes. This changed by 2000 when the first sub-degree programmes came under review by the HKCAA.

Thirdly, the widening scope of accreditation also meant that academic accreditation was no longer limited to the publicly funded institutions in Hong Kong which was the case before 1996. In 1996, Hong Kong Shue Yan College was the first private tertiary institution to engage the HKCAA to conduct academic accreditation and this was followed by another private institution, Caritas Francis Hsu College, in 2000. These changes came about as a result of the widening access to education and the government's recent policy of promotion of private education in Hong Kong (see below).

Table 2.2 shows a summary of the academic accreditation exercises conducted by the HKCAA between 1990–2000.

Guiding Principles of Academic Accreditation

The HKCAA promulgates the following guiding principles in its work of academic accreditation:

1) independence of the external quality assurance body The HKCAA is established as an independent statutory body, governed by an international council of academic and non-academic members. It functions independently of government and the funding bodies, formulates its own accreditation

Table 2.2 A summary of institutional reviews and course validations conducted by the HKCAA at Hong Kong education institutions

Institution	Number of institutional reviews	First year of institutional review	Number of validations and revalidations	Year of first validation	Year of acquiring self-accreditation status
Hong Kong Polytechnic	–	–	50	1990	1993
City Polytechnic of HK	–	–	35	1990	1993
HK Baptist College	1	1990	12	1990	1993
Lingnan College	1	1990	18	1990	1998
Open Learning Institute of Hong Kong	3	1990	5	1992	1996
HK Academy for Performing Arts	2	1991	13	1991	–
Colleges of Education*	1	1994	–	–	–
HK Institute of Education	2	1995	11	1995	–
HK Shue Yan College	1	1996	3	2000	–
Caritas Francis Hsu College	1	2000	2	2000	–

* Refers to the four Colleges of Education and the Institute of Language in Education that were merged to form the Hong Kong Institute of Education in 1994

Source: HKCAA Tenth Anniversary Publication 2000.

criteria and procedures, engages its own professional staff, and utilises independent consultants and academic experts in its work. The independent nature of the HKCAA and its operation ensures that the outcomes of accreditation are free from any political or policy/funding considerations. The results of academic evaluation represent the unbiased professional academic opinion of the Council, for the reference of the government, policy-makers, institutions, and the community.

Financially, the HKCAA is independent of the government and it draws its operating costs from fees charged to the commissioning organisations of the accredited institutions or the institutions themselves, and also other clients making use of the services of the Council;

2) respect for the autonomy of tertiary institutions external academic accreditation is carried out in accordance with the principle of academic autonomy of the tertiary institutions and respect for the rights of an institution to design programmes of study which are in line with its own mission and the programme objectives set by itself. The external accreditation body does not stipulate mandatory requirements in respect of course design or aspects of the courses and will evaluate the quality of the course in terms of its ability to meet its stated objectives and international standards at the same time;

3) promotion of institutional responsibility for quality The model of external academic accreditation practised by the HKCAA is based on the belief that the maintenance of the quality of educational provisions cannot solely depend upon external scrutiny but must also rest upon the awareness and self-discipline of the institution regarding the quality of its provisions. Thus institutions are urged to build up their own internal quality assurance systems and culture. It is the working principle of the HKCAA that institutions should be able, after a period of time, to reach a stage of maturity where they can be responsible for the quality of their individual programmes of study and are no longer required to undergo programme validations. However, this does not mean that there should no longer be any external scrutiny. Rather, the role of the external quality assurance body will have changed from micro management of the institutions through programme validation, to macro evaluation of the institutions and their quality assurance processes.

Academic Accreditation

'Academic accreditation' is defined in the HKCAA Ordinance as 'any evaluation, assessment or other activity to determine whether or not the academic standards of any institution of higher education are comparable with internationally recognized standards'.

Academic accreditation conducted by the HKCAA comprises 'institutional review' and 'programme validation'. Institutional reviews are defined in the HKCAA Ordinance as 'a review of the academic and general standards of an institution of higher education'. The purpose of an institutional review varies with the stage of development of an institution. For non-degree granting institutions, the purpose of an institutional review is to ascertain whether the academic environment of the institution is suitable for implementing degree programmes which have standards comparable with those recognised internationally. For institutions which already have degree-granting powers, the review will assess whether the institution continues to maintain a suitable academic environment for offering degrees. Alternatively, the review may be intended to assess the institutions' readiness to take full responsibility for the standard of its own programmes of study, that is, to achieve 'institutional accreditation' ('self-accreditation') status. 'Institutional accreditation' is defined in the HKCAA Ordinance as 'an assessment to determine whether an institution of higher education is competent to validate or revalidate ... degree courses conducted or proposed to be conducted by it.'

Institutional reviews therefore examine an institution's structures, organisation, and processes, its plans and resources, to form an assessment of the institution's capability and readiness to offer degree (or other) programmes. The issues generally considered in such a review include institutional structure, institutional governance and management, programme development and design, academic staff, scholarly activity, student admission and student services, programme evaluation and quality assurance, resources, collaboration and community links. The institution's development plans, its goals and missions are also considered in the review.

Programme validations are defined in the HKCAA Ordinance as 'an evaluation of a particular degree course conducted or proposed to be conducted by an institution of higher education, to determine whether or not the academic standard of the course is comparable with internationally recognised standards'.

Programme validations are conducted in respect of degree programmes that are proposed to be offered and therefore are usually conducted prior to any intake of students to the programme. Programme validations consider issues such as programme structure and design, teaching and learning, assessment, academic staff, facilities and support, staff development, quality assurance, links with the profession/industry, and any other issues having an impact on the quality of the programme.

The outcome of both institutional reviews and programme validation fall into the categories of (i) approval; (ii) non-approval; or (iii) approval with conditions and/or recommendations. It should be emphasised that the purposes of both institutional reviews and programme validations encompass an element of advice to the institutions, through the process of peer review and constructive dialogue. And finally through the setting of conditions and/or recommendations for improvement, the institution is encouraged and assisted to review and refine its plans in the light of international standards and good practices.

The *process* of institutional reviews and programme validations comprise the following elements:

- submission of documentation (often including a self-evaluation) from the institution;
- peer review process;
- site visit to the institution;
- a report to the commissioning body.

Usually a period of approval will be recommended, after which a follow-up review of the institution (in the case of institutional review), or a revalidation of the programme (in the case of programme validation) will be conducted.

Features of HKCAA Academic Accreditation

Academic accreditation conducted by the HKCAA is marked by the special features of international dimension, peer review, community participation, and holistic assessment.

International dimension and peer review The aim of academic accreditation in Hong Kong is to ensure that the standard of higher education is maintained at an international level so that the graduates from the education system can maintain a competitive edge on the international market and sustain a quality labour force for the vibrant economy of Hong Kong. The accreditations of the HKCAA are conducted by the use of international and local panels of subject and accreditation experts who are able to draw upon the experiences of their respective countries and international practice for the benefit of Hong Kong's higher education.

Community participation Input from the community is highly valued in the accreditation activities and members from the relevant profession or trade are normally included on review panels for the advice they can provide in respect of the community expectation of the type of graduates to be produced and the skills and competencies expected of graduates.

Holistic assessment Institutions and programmes are assessed using a holistic approach that takes into consideration a range of relevant factors having an impact on the quality of the institution or programme. There is as much emphasis on qualitative as on quantitative evaluation, and the institution/ programme study is viewed in totality for arriving at an overall outcome. Hence, sufficient flexibility is built into the system to allow for differences among institutions and also to take account of variations in international practices.

Post Institutional Accreditation/Self-Accreditation

Periodic review Following the principle of encouraging institutional maturity in the long term, as promulgated by the HKCAA, tertiary institutions which had been subject to external accreditation by the HKCAA worked towards building up their internal quality assurance systems and strove towards attaining the status of institutional accreditation (more commonly termed as self-accreditation). The scheme of self-accreditation envisages that even when institutions attain the status where they would be free from external validation of programmes, they should continue to be subject to some form of periodic external review, albeit at the macro level. This is in line with current international thinking that tertiary institutions should remain all the time accountable for their quality and be answerable to the community and to stakeholders and funding bodies.

The Open Learning Institute of Hong Kong that achieved self-accreditation status and later university status, was required by government to undergo external review by the HKCAA at five-yearly intervals, in respect of the quality assurance processes of the university. The first such review is due to be conducted in 2001/02.

Teaching and Learning Quality Process Reviews In respect of those institutions funded by the University Grants Committee which had been granted self-accreditation status, namely, the Hong Kong Polytechnic University, the City University of Hong Kong, the Hong Kong Baptist University, these were subject to external review by the UGC of the quality assurance of their teaching and learning processes. Interestingly, this review, termed Teaching and

Learning Quality Process Review (TLQPR), was also imposed upon those universities that had never been subject to any external accreditation. The first round of TLQPR, designed in consultation with a Consultative Committee formed of representatives from the institutions to be reviewed, was conducted in 1996. The exercise involved institutional self-evaluation and site visits by a team that comprised UGC members, institutional representatives, and members nominated by the HKCAA. The purpose of the exercise was to evaluate the quality assurance processes for teaching and learning in the institutions rather than the quality and outcome of teaching and learning themselves.

Institutional Autonomy vs External Quality Assurance

As more and more institutions were achieving self-accreditation status, the debate continued as to whether it is sufficient to leave the monitoring of quality entirely to the discretion of the self-accrediting institution, subject only to periodic reviews of their quality assurance processes. On the one hand, institutions guard their academic autonomy preciously and the self-accrediting institutions, in particular, claim that they should be free from any external monitoring of the quality of their educational provisions. On the other hand, educationalists noted that the community and employers are not entirely satisfied with the product of higher education, and in recent years there have been concerns voiced about the competencies of graduates when they enter the job market. There are schools of thought which feel that the monitoring of quality assurance processes in the institutions, as limited to an investigation about processes and stops short of the direct evaluation of the quality and outcomes of either study programmes or of students, may not be sufficient. The Reform Proposals for the Education System in Hong Kong, issued by the government in September 2000, report that most respondents in the consultation period agreed that 'the quality assurance mechanisms of universities should be strengthened'; and some suggested that basic assessments on Chinese, English and IT should be required by undergraduates. (Section 8.4.38) The Reform Proposals also posed the following propositions (Section 8.4.39):

- besides reviewing the learning and teaching quality assurance processes, should external assessments be conducted on the effectiveness of learning and teaching (such as the standards of graduates);
- how might the universities' self-accrediting mechanisms be strengthened?

This concern over quality was perhaps again reflected in government quarters when there was a decision made requiring the language proficiency training courses for teachers offered by the tertiary institutions (including self-accrediting institutions), to be subject to external review and approval, with assessment of the courses to be conducted by the HKCAA. Even though these are non-degree courses, the decision could be seen as signifying the government's concern for the quality of education and the need it sees for direct involvement in order to guarantee quality.

Institutions' Internal Quality Assurance

Degree-granting institutions in Hong Kong all have established internal procedures for the approval of the programmes they conduct. There is usually an approval process involving different levels such as departmental committees, faculty boards, and the Senate/Academic Board or an equivalent body that is the highest academic decision-making body in the institution.

The newer institutions which had been externally accredited by the HKCAA have developed internal validation procedures which are modelled on the external accreditation model, involving peer academic review which often involves the input of external subject experts and other external advisors. There is also a process of revalidation of the programmes at regular or specified intervals. Some institutions have additionally developed annual internal programme review cycles.

These quality assurance processes for the approval of courses or validation and monitoring of courses apply to the internal departments of the tertiary institutions. Most of the continuing education departments of the tertiary institutions follow different procedures of approval which are specific to these departments.

In the last few years most of the tertiary institutions underwent some form of internal review of their own quality assurance mechanisms as a result of the Teaching and Learning Quality Process Reviews (TLQPR) conducted by the University Grants Committee on the institutions under its remit. The first round of TLQPR was conducted in 1996. Both before the Process Reviews were conducted, and after the results were announced to the institutions, the institutions responded by undertaking reviews of their internal quality assurance mechanisms.

In the exercise, teaching and learning processes are described in terms of five sub-processes, namely, curriculum design, pedagogical design, implementation quality, outcome assessment and resource provision. The review panel suggested to the institutions that these different process dimensions may be approached from the perspective of four quality assurance methods, namely, quality programme framework, direct quality programme activities, quality programme support and values and incentives. However, it was emphasised that the institutions should define their own processes and that the suggested framework was not meant to be prescriptive.

After the first round of the exercise the reports were sent to the individual institutions. The institutions were encouraged to publish the reports and in the event of the first round, all reports had been published. The UGC is in the process of planning for the second round of TLQPR.

The tertiary institutions have also paid greater attention to the quality control of their research output as a result of the Research Assessment Exercises (RAE) conducted by the UGC, which assesses the number of active researchers in each institution as well as the quality of research, with the result being applied to guide the apportionment of recurrent research funding to the institutions.

Registration of Non-local Courses: the Non-local Higher and Professional Education (Regulation) Ordinance

Legislative Control

Control over the quality of higher education extended into the realm of non-local educational courses with the introduction of the Non-local Higher and Professional Education (Regulation) Ordinance in 1996.

Hong Kong has become a growing market for courses exported from overseas countries in the 1990s. Despite the expansion of local higher education and the availability of many part-time study opportunities through institutions such as the Open University of Hong Kong, and the continuing education departments of local universities, there seems to be an insatiable demand for post secondary education courses. Most of these are offered by English speaking countries and lead to academic awards ranging from sub-degrees, degrees, to postgraduate degrees from an overseas/non-local institution. A small number lead to professional awards from overseas/non-local professional bodies. By 1996, prior to the enactment of the Ordinance, unofficial sources estimate that there were at least 400 such courses operating in Hong Kong. These courses were not subject to any form of quality control and were able to make full use of the free market in Hong Kong, creating a wide spectrum of study opportunities and employing a wide range of teaching/delivery modes. Non-local institutions were free to promote their product and services in Hong Kong and there was no requirement for approval from the government. Increasingly there were concerns being raised over the quality of some of these courses. While it is the government's intention to maintain free trade and the free import of educational products into Hong Kong, eventually it decided it was necessary to introduce legislative control to ensure that substandard courses do not operate in Hong Kong and to offer a minimum level of consumer protection.

After a few years of planning, the Non-local Higher and Professional Education (Regulation) Ordinance was enacted in July 1996. Under the Ordinance all non-local educational and professional courses (regulated courses) which were already operating in Hong Kong were required to be registered by June 1998, and thereafter all new courses must be registered before they can legally operate. The Hong Kong Council for Academic Accreditation was appointed as the advisor to the Registrar of Non-local Courses to assess the registrability of the regulated courses according to the criteria stipulated under the Ordinance, and also to review the Annual Returns submitted by the non-local courses for their suitability to continue to be registered.

Under the Ordinance, regulated courses refer to:

> a course of education conducted in Hong Kong consisting of lectures, tutorials, seminars, group discussion sessions, instruction, or dissemination of information or materials or any combination of those elements which leads to the award of any non-local higher academic qualification or non-local professional qualification and includes, where the context admits, a proposed such course.

Distance learning courses which do not have a physical presence in Hong Kong are not required to be registered but may voluntarily apply to do so.

Courses which are operated in collaboration with those local tertiary institutions as listed in the Ordinance may apply for exemption from registration, while those operated by non-local institutions themselves or in partnership with other organisations in Hong Kong are required to apply for registration. Application for exemption entails a simpler process although the same criteria apply to registration and exemption under the Ordinance.

The criteria for registration/exemption of courses leading to a non-local post secondary *academic* awards require that:

1) the institution is a recognised non-local institution;
2) effective measures must be in place to ensure that the standard of the course is maintained at a level comparable with a course conducted by the institution in its home country leading to the same qualification; and
3) this comparability in standard must be recognised by the institution, the academic community in that country and the relevant accreditation authorities in that country (if any).

The criteria for registration/exemption of courses leading to non-local *professional* awards require that the particular course be recognised by the professional body making the award, and that the professional body be a recognised body for the relevant profession in the home country.

The courses applying for registration are assessed by the HKCAA in accordance with the stipulated criteria. For academic courses, the basic criteria relate to the comparability of the course offered in Hong Kong with the same course offered in the home country, and the existence of effective measures to ensure this comparability. There are no mandatory requirements as to what constitute 'effective measures' for maintaining and monitoring the quality of the courses. While an institution should have the autonomy to put in place measures which it regards as effective to uphold quality, particular attention will be paid to whether the overseas institution has overall control over its offshore courses and whether there are formal policies and systems for quality assurance and how these are implemented. Specifically, questions will be asked as to whether measures adopted by the overseas institution are effective in maintaining the quality of courses in Hong Kong at a comparable standard with the overseas course, having regard to the comparability of the programme content, modes and methods of delivery, assessment, staffing, and other teaching support. The underlying philosophy is that it is insufficient for an institution to profess statements or stated policies about the quality assurance procedures of their offshore operation. It is important that the quality assurance of the courses be demonstrated through their actual operation.

By November 2000, the HKCAA had conducted assessment on a total of 394 non-local courses, and recommended registration for over 90 per cent of them, many with conditions attached which require changes or improvement to their operation and quality measures. In addition, there are over 305 courses that have successfully applied for exemption. The total number of 621 courses on the market reveals that there is a continuing demand for higher education over the years. It underlines also the significance of the need for measures for monitoring the quality of these courses since they are educating a sizeable proportion of the population and workforce of Hong Kong as well as drawing sizeable fees from this student population.

Recognition vs Registration

The enactment of the Ordinance has attempted to introduce minimum standards for the operation of non-local courses, through ensuring that the educational courses offered in Hong Kong are at least comparable with the home courses. To maintain a wide range of consumer choice the government has deliberately avoided setting any stipulated standard for the non-local courses, either in accordance with international standards or a local benchmark. Both the government and the HKCAA are careful to emphasise that the registration/ exemption status of the non-local courses does not mean 'recognition' by the government or any employer, nor does it equal 'academic accreditation' by the HKCAA. Registration/exemption is the fulfilment of legislation requirements for operation of the courses and has no implication for the academic standard of the courses. Consumers are still required to exercise their discretion. The government requires all registered/exempted courses to carry a statement in their promotional materials stating that: 'It is a matter of discretion for individual employers to recognise any qualification to which this course may lead.'

Thus while the introduction of legislative control has striven to achieve a balance between a free market and the control of quality, it has not quite satisfied those parts of the community which have expectations for more guidance from the government or from the accreditation authority on the *quality* of the non-local courses. Potential students of the courses as well as employers are also keen to obtain assurances about the recognition of their qualification upon graduation from the non-local courses. While realising the difficulty of the task, the government is cognizant of this expectation from the public for an official pronouncement on the recognition of these courses. As a major employer in Hong Kong, the government is also deeply aware of the desirability of introducing a 'recognition' scheme for the non-local courses which is based on the standard of the courses per se.

As the only academic accreditation body in Hong Kong, and as the advisor to the government in the registration of the non-local courses, the HKCAA has been drawn into the discussion as to whether and how non-local courses may be assessed for their standards. Stemming from its role of accreditation, the HKCAA has gradually evolved a role in which it also proffers advice to the government and employers on the standard of overseas qualifications obtained by Hong Kong citizens studying abroad. It has over the years become the chief advisor to the government on the comparability of such qualifications with local standards, for purposes of civil service appointment. In pursuance of this role, the HKCAA might be working together with the government towards a scheme for the assessment of non-local courses offered in Hong Kong, to provide better information for the consumers and the employers of Hong Kong. There are different lines of thought on how the current registration process may be taken forward: whether there should be a process of accreditation to be initiated and sought by the non-local institutions; or whether it should be another government imperative to require academic accreditation or the fulfilment of stipulated standards as a condition of operation in Hong Kong. This debate raises once again the perennial issue of balance: between the free market and consumer protection, and between institutional autonomy and the external monitoring of quality.

Education Expansion and Implications for Quality

The 1980s had seen a vast expansion in the higher education system with the birth of new institutions and the upgrading of existing institutions to become degree-awarding. The 1990s saw a consolidation of this growth but also witnessed a rise in the provision of educational opportunities by non-local education coming to operate in Hong Kong. In the late 1990s the government emphasised the importance of a knowledge-based society to support the continuous growth and transformation of the economy.

In 1999 the Education Commission started to conduct a review of the entire education system of Hong Kong in order to formulate a system which can keep up with the environment and the needs of society in the twenty-first century. The overall direction of the education reform is to offer all-round and balanced learning opportunities, and to promulgate lifelong learning. The aims of education for the twenty-first century are formulated as follows in the *Reform Proposals for the Education System in Hong Kong*, issued in September 2000:

> To enable every person to attain all-round development in the domains of ethics, intellect, physique, social skills and aesthetics according to his/her own attributes so that he/she is capable of life-long learning, critical and exploratory thinking, innovating and adapting to change; filled with self-confidence and a team spirit; willing to put forward continuing effort for the prosperity, progress, freedom

and democracy of their society, and contribute to the future well-being of the nation and the world at large.

The proposed reforms span a wide range of areas in the education system, covering the academic structure of senior secondary school, the bachelor degree system, assessment mechanisms for schools, university admission mechanisms, teacher education, continuing education, and other issues. Among the various educational reforms being proposed, one of the aims is the expansion of educational opportunities. The *Reform Proposals* state that

> As a matter of fact, in many other parts of the world, the proportion of post-secondary places for the relevant age group far exceeds that in Hong Kong, which is only about 34%.
>
> What Hong Kong needs is a diversified education system which provides more learning opportunities at senior secondary level and beyond through different modes and system of learning.

Thus the educational reforms have as one of the aims the expansion of educational opportunities at the post-secondary level. This will be achieved, *inter alia*, through the encouragement of private higher education, the creation of community college-type of institutions, and the expansion of continuing education provision.

Until now there are no private higher education providers in Hong Kong which are authorised to conduct undergraduate level study. The Hong Kong Shue Yan College, which is a private registered Post Secondary College in Hong Kong became the first private institution to express interest in becoming a private degree-awarding institution. In order to ensure the quality of its educational provisions, the College was given funding by the government to engage the HKCAA to accredit its proposed degree programmes. In 2000 the HKCAA conducted a review of the College including its institutional environment and one of its degree programme proposals. Thus the College was the first private degree-granting institution to undergo accreditation by the HKCAA. This signified not only the start of private higher education in Hong Kong but also the government's concern for the quality of higher education as it expands into the private sector.

The Education Commission's *Reform Proposals* also raised the possibility of overseas institutions establishing private universities in Hong Kong, a phenomenon which has not yet happened in Hong Kong, nor had it been previously specifically encouraged. If this were to happen, issues of the quality assurance of private universities from outside Hong Kong would also need to be addressed.

An innovative development proposed by the Education Commission is the establishment of community colleges, which would offer sub-degree qualifications and are envisioned as providing learners with 'an alternative route to higher education that, to a certain extent, articulates with university programmes'. In addition they can provide 'a second opportunity to learners who have yet to attain qualifications at secondary level through formal education'. In response to these suggestions, a number of universities have initiated the development of 'associate degrees', either through the continuing education departments or internal departments of these universities. There is as yet no official definition of associate degrees, although the offering departments proclaim that these can eventually articulate with the degrees offered by the universities. These new developments throw up again the question of quality assurance of these new awards. The *Reform Proposals* state very clearly that there is a need for 'a sound mechanism for qualifications accreditation', and that the government should facilitate the establishment of a mechanism for quality assurance (Sections 8.4.52 and 8.5.8).

Qualifications Framework

This new spate of expansion in higher education has intensified the need to establish a Qualifications Framework for Hong Kong, to facilitate a clear definition of the different levels of qualifications and to enable the transfer and articulation of qualifications. The HKCAA, in a submission to the government in 1997, highlighted the desirability of setting up such a framework for Hong Kong, in line with the practice in many countries, to create a more coherent, understandable, and recognizable system of post secondary qualifications for Hong Kong and to establish a system of quality assurance for these qualifications. Similar concerns would have been voiced by other academic bodies in Hong Kong. In the *Reform Proposals*, the government identifies a particular need to set up a Qualifications Framework in the continuing education sector. The proposals also encourage the tertiary institutions to work towards 'a flexible and transferable credit unit system among institutions and departments'.

There is at present no system-wide transfer and recognition of credit at the degree level among the tertiary institutions. Individual institutions may institute mutual acceptance agreements between themselves but there are few instances of these and it is the norm for students to complete their study within one institution.

At the sub-degree level there is even less systematic transfer of credit. The myriad of post secondary/sub-degree qualifications that exist in Hong Kong has not been conducive towards any systematic recognition of these qualifications. As there is no limitation on the type of sub-degree qualifications which may be awarded, a large number of such qualifications entitled diplomas, higher diplomas, certificates, higher certificates, professional diplomas, advanced certificates, etc. have mushroomed in the territory. The more readily recognizable qualifications are those awarded by the publicly funded institutions: the former polytechnics and the universities, the Vocational Training Council, and registered Post-Secondary Colleges. But even among the qualifications awarded by these institutions there are differences in respect of entry requirements and exit standards even where the award has the same title. In addition, there are over 1,000 post secondary awards offered by the continuing education departments/schools of the tertiary institutions, and also numerous private institutions which award different qualifications among which there is even less consistency.

The *Reform Proposals* have encouraged the bringing together of various sectors 'to establish a comprehensive mechanism for accreditation of academic qualifications', and the setting up of 'a comprehensive mechanism whereby qualifications are mutually recognised and transferable among various continuing education/formal education/professional/vocational training programmes' (Sections 2.41 (5) and 8.57).

It would indeed be an extremely challenging task to set up a Qualifications Framework, if added to the existing scene of a large configuration of qualifications awarded by public and private institutions, there are the new qualifications of *associate degrees*; and on top of these, the sub-degree and degree level qualifications offered by non-local institutions in Hong Kong. Challenging as the task may be, both the government and the academic community see the urgent need to introduce a measure of consistency and quality control into this forest of qualifications both to provide an informed choice for students and employers, and to facilitate the articulation of qualifications and eventually the goal of lifelong learning.

Hong Kong started with a binary system in higher education more than ten years ago when the old university sector was automatically self-accrediting, while the new degree-granting polytechnic sector was subject to external accreditation. Over the years, with the new institutions being granted self-accrediting status, the binary system has not really disappeared as it has in the

UK; instead the binary line has merely shifted. There are newer degree-awarding institutions that continue to undergo external accreditation and that remain on the other side of the binary line.

The current education reforms that are spear-heading a growth in private post-secondary and higher education will help to perpetuate the binary system, with new private education providers possibly being subjected to more vigorous scrutiny of their programmes than the older established institutions; albeit that the latter undergo external scrutiny of their quality assurance processes through the TLQPR conducted by the UGC (for UGC funded institutions) or institutional reviews conducted by the HKCAA (for non-UGC funded institutions). But the latter is a scrutiny of processes rather than of standards and quality.

Behind the concept of the binary system is the assumption that as institutions become more mature, they should be entrusted with the quality control of their teaching and learning. However, stakeholders in different parts of the world are increasingly posing the question whether it is sufficient for the Government or funding body to monitor the process alone and whether or not there should be requirements for minimum standards. These questions involve issues of accountability where huge amounts of public money are being spent; they involve issues of the standard of graduates that the higher education system is producing for the economy. There are different schools of thought as to this relationship between the stage of maturity of an institution and its ability to monitor its own standards.

The UK system, from which Hong Kong has borrowed heavily for its accreditation and quality assurance system, has already moved away from the binary system and adopted a more comprehensive quality assurance model that embraces old and new institutions, that inspects systems as well as quality. What lesson can Hong Kong learn from this model that is also extant in many other parts of the world, including the US, Mainland China and parts of Europe?

There are also other schools of thought that distinguish between public-funded and private-funded institutions where quality assurance is concerned. Some would argue that public funded institutions can be trusted to maintain quality while the private for-profit providers should be carefully monitored. The other side of the argument is that there should be closer scrutiny where public money is involved, whereas private providers will only be able to survive market forces if they offer quality products. But then, is it possible to leave the quality of education to be determined solely by market forces? Are students/consumers able to make a wise choice? The growth in quality assurance agencies and the enactment of legislation by governments around the world underline the realisation by the peoples and the governments concerned that the quality of education and its upkeep is too important a matter to be left to market forces. As in many other walks of life where governments feel the need for regulations to protect the interests or safety of the citizens, the same imperative for government interference exists in education, irrespective of the nature of the educational institution.

Hong Kong is a society noted and valued for its diversity. The current direction is for post-secondary and higher education to move towards a more diverse system to include private providers and, in the future, private universities. To make this system understandable to the public and, more importantly, to maintain consistency in standard across the system, what is required is a more centralising quality assurance system that can do this job, that remains accountable to the government and to society and that is also firmly rooted in the local and educational system of Hong Kong. While it may be tempting to introduce a variety of quality assurance systems – as Hong Kong is always attracted to diversity and trends in globalisation is making this appear even more attractive – one should be cautioned against the havocs that will undoubtedly ensue if diversity is super-imposed upon diversity. We should thus be guarded against those destabilising forces that seek to trade quality for diversity and which, in the end, will undermine Hong Kong's efforts to maintain a quality education system and workforce.

References

Hong Kong Council for Academic Accreditation Handbook 1997/98.
Hong Kong Council for Academic Accreditation Ordinance, 1990.
Hong Kong Council for Academic Accreditation Tenth Anniversary Publication, 2000.
Hong Kong 1999, Government of Special Administrative Region, Hong Kong.
Learning for Life, Learning through Life: Reform Proposals for the Education System in Hong Kong, Education Commission, Hong Kong Special Administrative Region of The People's Republic of China, September 2000.
Leong, J. (2001), 'Free Market vs Quality: The Hong Kong Experience of Global Education', paper presented at the International Conference on New Millennium: Quality and Innovations in Higher Education, Hong Kong.
Non-local Higher and Professional Education (Regulation) Ordinance.
University Grants Committee of Hong Kong, China, Report for July 1995 to June 1998.
Wong, W.S. (1998), 'Academic Accreditation in Hong Kong: the Independent Accreditation Agency Model', in Dr Yuehluen Hu (ed.), *Research into Higher Education Accreditation in Mainland China*, Taiwan and Hong Kong (in Chinese).

Chapter Three

Quality Assurance and Evaluation of Higher Education in Mainland China

Xu Demin, Qi Suiyuan and Wang Runxiao
Northwestern Polytechnic University, Xi'an China

Higher Education Development in China

Higher education in China has a history of over a century following the foundation of the Zhongxi School in Tianjin during the Qing dynasty in 1895. Prior to 1949, higher education in China was slow to develop and small in scale with only 205 colleges and 7,110 registering students. It basically followed the example of, and drew, on the experience of models of higher education in western countries especially the UK and the USA. Since the foundation of the Peoples' Republic of China (PRC) there has been considerable development of, and achievement in, Chinese higher education and its management. The socialist system has encouraged the development of a system characterised with its own values and norms.

The Higher Education Law of the PRC of 1999 regularised the higher education system and its legal management so that higher education now comprises degree and non-degree education in both full-time and part-time modes. In addition, teaching by radio, television, correspondence and other forms of distance education have come to play a very important role in contemporary higher education. The system is categorised by junior college as well as undergraduate and graduate education. Following the Degree Regulation of the PRC (1981) three kinds of degree have been offered: bachelor, master and doctor. Twelve specialisms can be distinguished: philosophy, economics, law, education, literature, history, natural science, engineering, agriculture, medicine, military science (masters and doctorates only) and management, with 71 sub-disciplines and 249 majors in undergraduate education alongside 88 disciplines and 381 sub-disciplines in graduate education. In 1998, China had 1,984 colleges and universities comprising 1,022 that offered full-time courses and 962 adult education institutions. There are 6.2 million college students of whom 3.4 million are studying in the ordinary colleges and universities. Over 420 universities offer graduate education, among which 236 offer doctoral level education. Currently there are approximately 200,000 graduate students. Overseas students from over 150 different countries and regions study in 330 colleges and universities. About 1,500 have already been awarded master's degrees and 150 doctoral degree. Between 1998 and 2000 the number of enrolled students increased by 47 per cent. By 2010, the participation rate will have reached 15 per cent, thereby making higher education much more widely available than previously.

China is currently implementing two 'essential transformations' in its economic system and in the mode of economic growth by putting reform and 'opening-up' and the modernisation of socialism into a new era. This will lead to a new strategic objective, the development and reform of higher education in China. By around 2010, the aim is to establish a socialist higher education system with Chinese characteristics and to lay a solid foundation for the modernisation of higher education generally. The basic structure of the Chinese socialist higher educational system is:

1) the adherence to, and development of, the essential characteristics and advantages of socialist higher education;
2) the implementation of the strategy in order to develop higher education that is consistent with the environment in China and with an emphasis on size, structure and quality;
3) the establishment an energetic higher education and administration system that is adaptable to a socialist market economy;
4) the introduction of appropriate education and training opportunities in order to produce highly qualified graduates.

The Requirement of Quality (Norms) of Higher Education

In order to assure the quality of higher education and to cultivate able specialists, measures and requirements have been clearly provided through a series of regulations and laws such as the Higher Education Law, the Regulation of Academic Degrees, and the Catalogue of Subjects relating to education policy, the norms of professional ability, the length of schooling and the actual goals of education.

Education Policy

According to the Higher Education Law, higher education must conform to national education policy, serve the development of socialist modernisation and construction, apply knowledge to practice and provide an all-round development in terms of morality, intelligence and physique in the cause of socialist construction.

The norms of professional ability and length of schooling

- Junior college education should enable the student to master required basic theories and knowledge in his/her speciality and have the basic skills for jobs requiring this preliminary ability. The length of schooling is set at 2–3 years.
- Undergraduate education should enable the student systematically to master the required basic theories and knowledge in a particular speciality and provide the ability to do practical jobs and research work. The length of undergraduate education is set at 4–5 years.
- Graduate education should enable the student to master the more advanced theories in his/her branch of learning, provide systematic knowledge in his/her speciality and provide the corresponding skills, methods and relevant knowledge in order to undertake practical jobs and research work in the particular specialism. The length of graduate education is set at 2–3 years.
- Doctoral education should enable the student to display all the requirements of graduate education but at a more theoretical level and, at the same time, provide the ability to undertake creative research work. Typically, doctoral studies last 3–4 years.

According to the *Catalogue of Subjects* for undergraduate and postgraduate education clear and concrete regulations and requirements have been devised for all levels of higher education covering the education and training objectives and norms, the scope of the professions and their requirements, curriculum design and teaching procedures.

Quality Assurance of Higher Education in China

Since the priority of higher education is to foster superior specialisms, when it comes to students' education and training it is quality that becomes the key feature of higher education. Two aspects of quality assurance in higher education must be stressed: first, the supervision of quality from government and the Educational Administration Department and, second, quality assurance and its procedures within the particular college and university. The latter is subject to external scrutiny and provides a lifeline for the continued existence and further development of the college and university.

Teaching Quality Assurance within the College and University

The Higher Education Law states that the teaching quality in the universities must satisfy the government-established norms. Teaching activities are the essential method for student education and training in universities and thus their quality provides the essence and core of higher education. In this way a quality-assured system has to have been established for teaching evaluation in order to assure and improve education quality continuously. This is achieved in the following ways:

- there are four basic requirements of the comprehensive teaching quality assurance of student education. First, the integration of the all-round development of morality, intelligence, physique and individuality; second, the integration of human spirit and scientific competence; third, the integration of general and specialised knowledge; and last, the integration of the transmission and application of culture;
- there are two basic aspects of the quality assurance of the student education. The first relates to the whole process from enrolment to graduation. The second relates to the assurance of the quality of the student admission procedures and the provision of qualified teaching, learning and living services. These two processes of education and service complement each other since they have the same target in assuring the quality of student education;
- each department, each member of the academic staff, each procedure of education and teaching and all administrative staff combine to strengthen the consciousness of quality and to put quality assurance into practice;
- society requires that a sound system be established for tracking the careers and whereabouts of graduates. Surveys are also undertaken with employers. The feedback information undoubtedly helps improve the work and the quality of student education.

The teaching quality assurance system within the university The teaching quality assurance system within the university comprises the following four characteristics:

- *the objective*: the system is aimed at determining the appropriate scientific objective of each department, of each procedure in education and teaching and each member of staff in order to establish that the system is achieving its objectives. This is a key element of the system, for it is through this that education evaluation can include judgements that become the starting point (and the destination) for teaching quality assurance;
- *the execution*: in order to realise the objective successfully, universities have to establish a powerful executive and management system, education and teaching system and educational services system. The main task of management is to organise, plan, coordinate and supervise the implementation of the objective. The education and teaching system is the core and principal part of the executive system since it implements the objective by carrying out the actual education and teaching activities. The main task of the services system is to ensure the implementation of the objective, both spiritually and materially. In order to make this implementation programmable, standardised and scientific, an elaborate policy and regulation system has to be established;
- *the evaluation*: according to the quality requirement of student education, a scientific, feasible, simple and easy evaluation system needs to be established in order to collect the important information on education and teaching. This, after all, is the key to the value judgement as to how much the objective has been achieved in the quality of the student training on the basis, of course, of the evaluating norms. Such a system helps the administration system make decisions with regard to the improvement of quality;
- *the information*: the information system presents on-line information about the situation of each department and it's teaching procedures along with the feedback from graduates and employers. This helps in the analysis and judgement so as to highlight any departure from the stated objective and enables management to take corrective actions. The information system consists of two parts: one is internal to the universities, while the other is external. To supervise and assure the quality more efficiently advanced technology is often applied to build the network and information centre.

Emphasising the quality assurance of teaching Teachers in universities themselves play an important role in ensuring and improving the teaching quality since they are at the core of the system. Higher education in China has adopted a policy of teacher qualification so that only those with the appropriate qualification can be offered a teaching position. The Higher Education Law has clear requirements relating to ideology, morality, degree status and teaching ability. A university teacher qualification is approved by either the administrative department or authorised universities. This is a universally-accepted qualification that enables an academic to be employed by any of the universities.

There are two ways of evaluating the quality of teaching in the university. One is the evaluation carried out by students at the end of a particular course. The other is the process evaluation, in which the teacher's conduct in the teaching process is evaluated based on certain defined standards in order to estimate the teaching quality. The latter is widely adopted while the former, due to its limitation, is seldom used. The Universities Teaching Evaluation Table is constituted according to the main features of conduct in teaching. In this way teaching quality is evaluated by informed specialists and students.

External quality supervision of higher education To ensure that adequate quality is maintained in colleges and universities, controls from the government and society exist in addition to the internal quality assurance systems. Government lays down specific requirements and evaluation criteria for teaching standards in the colleges. Through a series of laws, rules and regulations relating to higher education, government also supervises various administrative measures such as the approval, verification, recording and inspection of higher education institutions. Evaluation of education and teaching quality is the key way of supervising and promoting the teaching level and ensuring its quality. The main characteristics of supervision are to examine higher education with respect to society as a whole and its requirements, to understand that the development of higher education relates closely to social development and to control the development of specific disciplines through the funding mechanism. It should be recalled, of course, that the supervision of quality comes directly from society, its demands and its needs. Following the introduction of a market economy system in China and the move towards greater delegation for the colleges and universities the government now attaches greater importance to 'social supervision' as a way of ensuring and improving the higher education quality in the longer term.

Government and society generally may implement their supervision in the following two ways: direct supervision and indirect supervision. Direct supervision refers to the supervision of the whole education system, while indirect supervision refers to the evaluation and supervision of educational quality through the use of a variety of social agencies.

Investment in higher education to ensure and enhance education quality To promote the reform and the development of higher education, investment in higher education has to be increased to meet various requirements. These investments arise mainly from government funding. Statutorily, it is now agreed that government will gradually increase its funding to ensure that steady and predictable funds flow into the government-supported colleges and universities. Education in China currently consumes 4 per cent of gross national product or 15 per cent of total financial expenditure. There is confidence in the PRC that such percentages will be at least maintained in the future if not actually increased. The government attaches great importance to the roles of macro-controls enacted by the means of financial allocation and makes a clear difference in terms of financial standards and methods between different levels and categories of colleges and universities. Thus, the founders of 'social-supported' colleges and universities know clearly their obligations as far as running arrangements, their institutional constitutions, and, especially, their financial obligations. Meanwhile the government is now encouraging higher education investment from, amongst others, business enterprises and even individuals.

Evaluation of Higher Education of China

Although a form of educational assessment system in China can be traced back to ancient times, the current education evaluation system started and developed gradually after universal student recruitment system resumed in 1977. Not until 1983 did the former Education Department officially lay down that colleges and universities should be evaluated. Following this announcement evaluation of colleges and universities flourished. In May 1985, the 'decision on reform of the education system' was made by the Central Committee of the Communist Party of China. This decision clearly stated that education levels of colleges and universities had to be evaluated while the powers of self-determination of the institutions should be simultaneously increased. This brought about a widespread development of evaluation activities. In October 1990, the National Education Committee issued the 'Temporary Regulations of Education Evaluation of General Colleges and Universities'. This regulation specifies as its key purpose the basic obligation and forms of evaluation along with their means of organisation and implementation. In February 1993, the Central Committee of the Communist Party, together with The State Council, published the 'Outline of Reform and Development of Chinese Education' that defines the central aim of the educational system reform as being to adapt to the needs of a socialist market economy along with defining the status and roles of relevant education evaluation.

In March 1995, the 'Education Law of the PRC' was approved at the 3rd session of the 8th People's Congress Council. The Law stipulates that the State takes responsibility for and implements the evaluation system for educational institutions. In August 1998, the Higher Education Law of the PRC, approved at the 4th session of the 9th Standing Committee of People's Congress Council, decided that the determination of education standards and the teaching quality of colleges and universities should be under the control of the Education Service and should be evaluated by it. In this legislative way the evaluation position of education, and higher education in particular, in China has been established in recent years. Over a 20 year period notable achievements have been attained in the evaluation of higher education, among which there are:

- a series of nationwide academic conferences on the theme of the evaluation of colleges and universities have been held along with a considerable number of large-scale evaluation training activities that have promoted a common understanding of educational evaluation and have prompted the development of theory that underpins evaluation;
- a series of theory-based research projects of education evaluation, external intercourse and cooperation activities have been undertaken that improve the level of theory research and practice activities of higher education evaluation and reduce the gap between China and the rest of the world;
- a series of books on the theory of education evaluation have been published together with many research papers that apply theory to practice. These have proved to be immensely popular and have done much in raising the awareness and knowledge of evaluation theory, the enhancement of its guidance into practice and a general overall improvement of the whole system;
- evaluation work with Chinese characteristics has been guaranteed a mandate and will lead eventually to further legislation guaranteeing it;
- the management and practice of higher education evaluation have been systematised and normalised providing a further step in ensuring the steady and profound development of evaluation in China.

The Quality Assurance and Evaluation of Higher Education in China

The issuing of the 'Temporary Regulation of College and University Evaluation' has led to three basic forms of evaluation – eligibility evaluation, 'optimisation' evaluation and institutional evaluation of colleges and universities.

Eligibility evaluation Eligibility evaluation assesses institutions or programmes according to basic threshold standards and the assessment usually involves an approval process. The major types of this form of assessment are:

- Accreditation for awarding postgraduate qualifications: the approval of institutions to conduct postgraduate programmes is the responsibility of the Academic Degrees Committee (ADC) of the State Council. Institutions must obtain approval prior to their application to award individual master's and doctoral programmes. A review process by subject discipline groups formed under the ADC is conducted at periodic intervals to assess the applications. Much of the evaluation work is conducted through the Institution for the Evaluation of Academic Degrees and Graduate Education (EADGE) established under the supervision of the Office of the ADC. In recent years, the approval of new master's degrees has been delegated to the provincial authorities in parts of China.
- Qualifying accreditation of new institutions established after 1978: this is a project conducted by the Ministry of Education to accredit those higher education institutions established after 1978 and also institutions that were upgraded to degree-awarding status in the 1980s, mostly institutions empowered to award bachelor rather than postgraduate qualifications. Institutions have to meet threshold standards in order to pass the accreditation.
- Evaluation of newly established institutions and programmes: this evaluation is carried out by relevant educational governing bodies (appointed by the Ministry of Education) when a new college and university is authorised and has its first intake of students. The eligibility benchmark of institutional quality is based on the Temporary Regulation whilst the eligibility standard of educational quality is based on the regulation relating to degree-awarding powers and related educational aims and specifications in the Degree Regulation of the PRC. When new programmes are being established, the application and approval process is normally conducted at the provincial level.

- Accreditation of Graduate Schools: after the establishment of Graduate Schools in 33 institutions in the 1980s, which comprise 44 per cent of doctoral programmes in Mainland China, a comprehensive evaluation was undertaken of these graduate schools starting in 1994 to assess their academic standard. The review was undertaken by the IEADGE under the supervision of the Office of the Academic Degrees Committee.

Optimisation evaluation Optimisation evaluation is a kind of appraisal and selection activity in higher education establishments aiming to identify and support excellence and to facilitate overall improvements.

The major types of optimisation evaluation are:

- Identification of institutions of excellence: this is a nationwide assessment exercise with voluntary participation in the assessment of outstanding achievement in undergraduate teaching. A pilot project was carried out in 1997 and formal assessment began in 1999. No ranking of institution will result from the assessment but institutions will be regarded as having passed the test.
- Selection of institutions for the P211 Project : this was conducted by the State Education Commission's P211 Office, together with assistance from the P211 Office set up inside provincial departments of education. The purpose is to identify and invest in 100 universities so that these can aim to be world-class or advanced institutions in China by the twenty-first century.

The assessment is done on the basis of applications from the universities together with support from the funding/supervising authority, pledging financial investment for the institution. A two-stage assessment involving site visits was carried out, organised by the SEC, assessing institutions on their self-report and plans of development.

Evaluation of institutions' organisation, management, and teaching Evaluation of an institution assesses institutions' organisation, management, teaching, etc. This evaluation takes place at regular intervals, normally every four or five years. The report of an evaluation will affirm achievements, point out weaknesses and make suggestions for improvement.

There are other single item evaluation carried out by different authorities including provincial education commissions, and ministries which fund higher education institutions, and each of these may serve different purposes. The evaluation may target a group of mono-discipline institutions under the same ministry, or a selective number of subject disciplines, or single items such as the comparative evaluation of library provision etc. The single evaluation is a comparative one, aiming to diagnose educational standard.

Characteristics of Higher Education Evaluation in China

Over time, the aim is to move from the rather centralised role of government through to a system whereby delegated evaluation powers are awarded to the individual institutions. Increasingly, also, experience and methodologies from overseas are being noted and incorporated into the Chinese system while at the same time recognising that the emergent system requires particular Chinese characteristics if appropriate reform is to take place. The higher education evaluation system is changing and developing rapidly, responding, in a sense, to the rapidly changing nature of Chinese society. As such it is to be expected that new methods of evaluation will be introduced almost on a continuous basis. Recent evidence demonstrates that evaluation is not simply being undertaken for assessment purposes *per se* but as a genuine means of improving the quality of delivery systems.

Distance-learning Higher Education and Sub-degree Education in China

In order to implement the strategy of becoming a more prosperous country through the development of science and education and by embracing the knowledge economy era, China has developed distance-learning delivery of higher education. Since the 1980s, China has developed a radio and television based college as well as correspondence colleges to offer higher education via education channels, audiovisual textbooks and the Internet in an attempt to open up higher education to a much wider constituency. The success of this is demonstrated by the fact that over two million students have graduated through this form of higher education already. In July 2000, the Ministry of Education authorised 31 key universities to establish networked educational institutes and to develop experimental contemporary distance teaching. This is a major development for higher education in China and is a further example of the move towards providing universal provision. The main tasks of these networked educational institutes are to develop degree and sub-degree education, to explore networked modes of teaching and to develop complex national networks. The selected 31 universities have been given considerable autonomy with regard to the recruitment of students, the development of teaching plans, the choice of teaching modes and the actual award of diplomas and degrees.

References

'The Law of Higher Education of the People's Republic of China', enacted in January 1999.
'The Degree Regulation of the People's Republic of China', enacted in January 1981.
'Outline of reform and development of education in China' (1993), The Centre of the Chinese Communist Party, Beijing: The State Council.
'Conferment of doctor, postgraduate degree and the brief introduction of discipline major of training postgraduates' (1999), Degree Committee Office of the State Council, Beijing: Higher Education Press.
'Undergraduate course major catalogue and brief introduction of general colleges and universities' (1998), Higher Education Department of the Ministry of Education, Beijing: Higher Education Press.
Wang Jisheng (2000), *Macro-pedagogy of Higher Education*, Beijing: Higher Education Press.
Wang Jisheng (2000), *The Higher Education of China in the 21st Century*, Beijing: Shaanxi People's Education Press.
Wu Bensha (2000), *Collected Works of Degree and Postgraduate Education*, Beijing: Xi'an Jiaotong University Press.
Xia Tianyang (1997), *Evaluation of Higher Rducation of the World*, Shanghai: Shanghai Science and Technology Literature Press.
Zhou Yuanqing (1999), 'Be ready for the 21st century: the reform and development of higher education of China', *Production and Study Co-operative Education*, 3, 4.

Chapter Four

Towards a European Dimension

Marie-Odile Ottenwaelter
Centre international d'études pédagogiques

Tradition and innovation are two factors that Europe has constantly had to come to terms with and one example is the evaluation of higher education. On the one hand, Europe can rely on a long university tradition since universities such as Bologna, Paris Sorbonne and Oxford, date back to the thirteenth century. Given this fact the power of history makes it more difficult to undertake any attempts at achieving harmonisation between countries with highly varying sizes, languages, cultures and legislative frameworks. Yet over the last 30 years higher education systems have undergone significant changes in terms of both their size and nature. The evaluation of higher education, which is rooted in these huge upheavals, is a new development in Europe.

Politically, the 'new' Europe is still under construction. Here we are chiefly concerned with the European Union, which is currently made up of 15 states and, along with those countries that are part of the free trade area, it corresponds to Western Europe.[1] The European Union is however in the process of being enlarged again and 13 countries, largely from Central and Eastern Europe have applied to become Member States.[2] It is therefore a very complex entity, in which its make up, its political structures and its thrusts are all under development.

In quantitative terms, the European Union is in many ways a unit comparable to the United States or Japan. It had in 1997, for example, a population of 291 million (almost 500 millions including those states which have applied for membership) whilst the USA has 269 million and Japan 126 million. Its percentage of the world wealth is 23.1 per cent, that of the USA 24.3 per cent and that of Japan 15.3 per cent. In the European Union there are around 12 million students (taking Europe in its largest sense that number rises to 15 million).

In this evolving Europe, it has been possible, within higher education, to observe the progression from the simple exchange of information (in order to improve mutual knowledge of each other's situation), the reinforcement of collaboration between Member States, the harmonising of systems and practices (for example in the area of courses and qualifications) to the final search for a European identity. This progression has been particularly evident in the field of quality assurance.

First Steps to Quality Assurance

Apart from the United Kingdom, which has a tradition of evaluation, based on accountability, dating back to 1917, other European countries did not introduce the systematic evaluation of higher education until recently. This can be explained by various factors.

Up to the 1970s what were the principal traits of European higher education? First and foremost it was public or state education. Private education, whenever it existed, was mostly based on religion, and it was chiefly non-profit making in nature. Generally speaking, education, whether basic or post-secondary, was viewed as a public good, apart from certain sectors such as management, art, design, and especially continuing education. The role of the state was therefore paramount, in recognising these establishments (the designation of the title 'university' being controlled) and the qualifications they awarded, as well their finances. Within this context two traditions developed, with one being based on university autonomy and the other on national centralisation, sometimes linked to a federal structure – the most significant examples of these two positions are the United Kingdom and the Netherlands, on the one hand, and France, Sweden and Spain on the other. Education, within universities, was first based on research and the main criteria for quality were to be found in the field of research, i.e. the evaluation of results and teams but also the evaluation of people – in other words the scientific quality of researching teaching staff, notably during recruitment and promotion; above all since the 1950s researchers had understood that the evaluation of research could only take place at an international level.

Since the 1970s all European countries have one after the other experienced huge changes in higher education with a substantial increase in the number of students following the introduction of mass higher education, which in turn also led to new profiles of students entering universities. New universities were created and many of them opened branches campuses in order to ensure that education was close at hand. Depending on the country this expansion was accompanied by an increase in finances or had to be run within the context of a restricted budget. Besides, universities took on a professional mantel and diversified their courses while enhancing internationalisation with the development towards greater mobility.

Given the sheer size of expenditure and the increasing complexities of institutions it soon became necessary to put in place evaluation procedures that would make it possible to verify that public funds were being used in the correct way, to guarantee the quality of education being offered to the younger generation and to guide the institutions. In the 1980s, the issue of evaluation was developed further so that it was not just a question of traditional *accountability* procedures but also one of new forms of *quality assurance*, aiming at improving institutions, both in terms of their policies and the way in which they were run. This time attention was paid to the quality of teaching and learning, thus counterbalancing the emphasis which had until then been placed on research.

The first quality assurance systems created reflected the diversity of the higher education systems to which they were applied and also the size of the countries concerned:

- the University Grants Committee in the United Kingdom set up the Academic Audit Unit in 1991 with a view to ensuring that universities, that benefit from extensive autonomy, had actually introduced all the quality assurance procedures required, and the Council for National Academic Awards (CNAA), in 1964, in order to assess the polytechnics;
- the *Comité National d'Evaluation* in France was created in law in 1984 and began by assessing one university after the other, institutionally, before carrying out parallel evaluations of disciplines and courses;
- beginning in 1988 the VSNU in the Netherlands carried out cross disciplinary evaluations which subsequently were completed by the evaluation of research and of institutions;
- the *Evalueringscenteret* in Denmark, created in 1992, also began by evaluating programmes.

It should be noted that this work has been carried out by the state and higher education institutions working together, with an emphasis on international openness. Yet other stakeholders such as businesses, financial backers and even the students have not really been involved.

European Initiatives

Given that the quality of higher education had become a major question at international level, the European Commission,[3] after the idea of creating a European Evaluation Agency (suggested in 1991 by the Dutch Presidency) had been put forward by Member States, took the initiative by launching a large pilot project, entitled the European Pilot Project for the Evaluation of Quality in Higher Education. This project ran from 1994 to 1995 and involved 17 countries. Its main aims were to highlight the need for evaluation in higher education; to enrich the evaluation procedures at national level; to encourage the exchange of experiences and; to give evaluation a European dimension. It is important to note that this project did not seek to rank or compare those institutions that were assessed, and above all that it did not aim to create a single system of evaluation for Europe, but it did aim to develop simultaneously in each country a culture of evaluation by testing a common method that could be adapted at the national level.

This method, which was the subject of *Guidelines*, was based on principles that were common to the four systems of evaluation that already existed in the United Kingdom, Denmark, France and The Netherlands:

- autonomy of the evaluation process from both governments and institutions;
- self evaluation;
- external review visit;
- public evaluation report.

The project focused on the evaluation of teaching while also taking into account the impact of research activities; it concentrated on two major disciplines (engineering, on the one hand, and, information and communication sciences or art/design, on the other). It focused on both the university and non-university sectors. It resulted in 46 self-evaluation reports, 46 evaluation reports (published in two languages),[4] 18 national reports (with the Flemish and French speaking communities in Belgium each submitting a report), and finally a European report.[5]

This means that it was possible to carry out a first common project within a short time, involving a large number of countries which, for the most part, had no experience in the field, thus offering them on the job training. It achieved a heightening of awareness to the problems of quality assurance, whether at institutional level or with regard to political authorities. It brought about numerous exchanges, acting as the embryo for the setting up of a network of different national evaluation experts. Finally, it makes it clear that, if common principles could be applied, cultural, legislative, linguistic, historical specificity – in short the 'national context' – would still nevertheless play an important role and that general principles must be adapted, translated and specified in order to correspond to national and regional realities.

Almost all the Member States then acted very quickly in setting up an evaluation system and creating their own agencies, or by at least forming a legislative framework or carrying out experiments. This is articulated in the report produced by *Evalueringscenteret* (Denmark) in September 1998, in conjunction with the *Comité National d'Evaluation* (France). The report,[6] relying on contributions from different countries, presents a comparative analysis of methods used to evaluate higher education and provides an overall picture of external evaluation procedures, country by country. This state-of-the-art illustrates great diversity, particularly as regards the following points:

- the university and non-university sectors sometimes operate the same system of evaluation (as in Finland and Portugal) and sometimes have two distinct systems (as in Belgium, Ireland and The Netherlands);
- the approach chosen may be institutional (as in France, Spain and the United Kingdom) or it may be disciplinary (based on disciplines, as is the case in The Netherlands, or on programmes, as is the case in the United Kingdom and Denmark);
- there are often two objectives, aiming both to improve quality and to control institutions but, depending on the case, priority is given to *accountability*, as is the case in the United Kingdom or to *improvement*, as is the case in France; certain countries, where the whole culture of quality assurance is already deeply rooted, carry out *audits* (as is the case in the United Kingdom and Sweden);
- evaluation may focus on education (both teaching and learning) or it may also take into account research, as well as the management of institutions;
- the importance of the regional dimension is emphasised in those countries that operate a type of federal system (such as Germany, Spain and, to a certain degree, the United Kingdom). Regional initiatives have also been developed by neighbouring countries (such as in Scandinavia) and by neighbouring regions from separate countries (such as those between The Netherlands, Flemish-speaking Belgium and Lower Saxony);
- in almost every case, the cost of self-evaluation is met by the institution while the cost of external evaluation is met by the agency, which itself benefits from public funding.

It is also possible to pick out one initiative that does not emanate from the States, nor from national organisation: the programme of institutional reviews from the CRE – Association of European Rectors. In fact, since 1994 the CRE has produced around 50 institutional reviews in some 20 European countries. These evaluations have been carried out by rectors and former rectors and their aim has been to assist those responsible for universities by helping them to improve the way in which the institutions are managed (notably by adapting to change) and to contribute to the promotion of a quality assurance culture. The cost of a review is currently around 25,000 Euros and is charged to the university that requests it.[7]

Another consequence of the Pilot Project, this time at a European level, is the Recommendation issued in September 1998 by the Council of the European Union.[8] This Recommendation – on *European Cooperation in Quality Assurance in Higher education* – is addressed at Member States, asking them to 'support and, where necessary establish transparent quality assurance systems' and to base systems of quality assurance on the principles of the Pilot Project. Together with the Commission, they are also encouraged to 'promote cooperation between the authorities responsible for quality assessment or quality assurance in higher education and to promote networking'.

In Central and Eastern Europe, a similar initiative has been introduced along the lines of the Pilot Project, and has been established within the framework of the Phare Programme.[9] The Project, *Quality Assurance in Higher education*, 1997/98, supported by the European Commission, involved 12 countries[10] and consisted of 11 evaluations of institutions and 17 evaluations of programmes. The project resulted in three publications: *A Legislative Review and Needs Analysis of developments in Central and Eastern Europe*,[11] a *Manual of Quality Assurance: Procedures and Practices* and; the *Final Report and Project Recommendations*.[12] In these countries the 1990s witnessed the move towards institutional autonomy, making it more and more necessary to introduce quality assurance mechanisms – notably in terms of accreditation. However, these mechanisms have often been put in place in a confused and sometimes conflicting manner. One of the main objectives of the project has therefore been the establishment of a feeling of trust between the different parties involved including governments, higher education managers and academic staff but also students, employers and society in general.

Finally, by applying the 1998 Recommendation and by extending the informal network, that has been in place since 1995, the Commission has supported the official creation of ENQA – *the European Network for Quality*

Assurance. The aim of this network is to promote cooperation *in* the field of quality evaluation and quality assurance. Its objectives are to encourage and develop the exchange of information and experience, to fulfil the request for expertise and advice on the part of the authorities in European countries, to support higher education institutions that wish to cooperate the field of quality assurance on a transnational basis and to promote contacts with international experts. The network is open to recognised quality assurance agencies, to public authorities responsible for quality assurance, and also to three European organisations, the CRE (the Association of European Universities), the Confederation of European Union Rectors Conferences and EURASHE (the European Association of Institutions in Higher Education). It covers the Member States of the European Union, EFTA countries and countries associated with the Community programmes on education and training.

The network held its first General Assembly in March 2000 and elected a steering group of eight members for three years, chaired by Christian Thune (Denmark). The network currently has 28 members. The evaluation agency in Finland is its secretariat. Its budget comes from membership fees (fixed at 1000 Euros a year) and from a grant from the European Commission. ENQA has its own website[13] and publishes a newsletter; it regularly organises workshops (for example, those on institutional evaluation, on self-evaluation at school or faculty level for staff members of Higher education and on follow up activities). It has been decided to participate in the Bologna follow-up (see below). The network does not take part in any accreditation process but it does play a moral role.

At the end of the 1990s, the European quality assurance situation was therefore characterised by considerable dynamism, with the setting up of new systems in most countries even though there was some confusion since national dynamics were not always convergent, or synchronised. European effort, as translated into the initiatives launched and supported by the Commission, has therefore chiefly consisted of encouraging Member States and higher education institutions to introduce quality assurance mechanisms and to develop exchanges between those responsible for quality assurance within the different countries in order to improve mutual knowledge and to move towards a certain harmonisation of practices. Yet, despite its willingness, the Commission is limited by European legislation that, in the area of education and training, places the initiative in the hands of the Member States. In the name of the principle of subsidiarity, the Member States keep the competences they are in a position to exercise themselves, and only those powers which they are not able to carry out to a satisfactory level are passed on to the Community.

Towards a European Dimension

The following initiative emanated from the Member States with the Sorbonne Declaration of May 1998 aiming at developing a European higher education arena. On the occasion of the 800th anniversary of the University of Paris, the French Minister for Education put forward a proposal to his colleagues from Germany, Italy and the United Kingdom suggesting developing the structure of their respective higher education systems in order to enable easy mutual recognition of qualifications, while respecting national specificities. The aim – to 'harmonise the structure of the European system of higher education' – was a response to the need to create a 'European dimension within higher education' – as a key way to promote citizens' mobility and employability and the continent's overall development.

A year later this trend had gained in momentum, since the Bologna Declaration[14] (19 June 1999) was signed by 29 countries. Given the need to enhance the competitiveness and attractiveness of the European higher education system, the signatories agreed to achieve several objectives by the year 2010. These objectives include the 'readability' of qualifications, the harmonisation of courses, the introduction of a system of credits (European Credit Transfer Scheme (ECTS)), the promotion of mobility but also 'the promotion of European cooperation in the field of quality assurance, as regards the drawing up of criteria and comparable methods' and 'the promotion of a necessary European dimension in higher education'. Working documents produced for the Bologna Conference open up ambitious prospects:

- compatible quality assurance systems, especially regarding the setting of threshold standards based on learning acquired (outputs) rather than on time spent and curriculum contents (inputs);
- independent evaluation leading to European quality labels in broad subjects areas;
- the current vacuum for independent evaluation in Europe would best be filled through agencies independent from national and European authorities, and working along subject lines;
- they could draw on existing and future European-wide subject-based networks;
- a coordinated approach to quality standards for transnational education, which raises the question of the recognition of foreign private providers.

Among the preparatory work undertaken let us mention three studies that have been carried out by higher education institutions with the support of the

Commission and cover respectively the follow-up and implementation of the Bologna Declaration, Accreditation and Transnational Education (TNE). The study on TNE aimed to analyse and make recommendations on the development and impact of transnational education on higher education in Europe. Member States (apart from the United Kingdom) are quite unfamiliar with the concept of TNE, if not totally rejecting the idea; but they are led to become conscious of the increasing importance of this phenomenon and of its existence in Europe. The ministers will have to consider several aspects, especially the question of protecting the consumer and therefore the measures to be taken in order to guarantee the quality of education and training on offer, whether it be imported or exported and also the role these new educational methods should play in the construction of a competitive European higher education arena.

Another study looks at accreditation – in the sense of state recognition of institutions, or even programmes, knowing that European standards have not been defined and that the primacy of political authorities at national level is maintained. Some options will be proposed to the Ministers involving the establishment of networks and institutional, bilateral and multilateral systems, in order to achieve mutual recognition. To the extent that these proposals have come from the institutions themselves, the recognition put forward is that of institutions rather than qualifications. The idea of a platform, making it possible to link institutional recognition and programme accreditation, is also envisaged but it is still at the working stage.

Yet initiatives have already been taken in that direction, notably emanating from higher education institutions, in the fields of management and engineering. In 1997, EFMD (European Foundation for Management Development), a non-profit European network of stakeholders in management education (uniting business schools, universities, large corporations, consultancies) introduced a system of certification called EQUIS, rather than letting the American AACSB (International Association of Management Education) extend an accreditation monopoly to Europe. Since then, EFMD and AACSB have reached an agreement to achieve mutual recognition. The EQUIS system has so far accredited 41 institutions, several of which are not European, such as the Business School of the Hong Kong University of Science and Technology. Similarly, a group of partners from higher education institutions in seven European countries (Finland, France, Germany, Italy, The Netherlands, Spain and Sweden) and representatives from the business world, Chambers of Commerce and Industry, Eurocadres and BEST (European Association of Students in Engineering) have become involved in the Leonardo

Project,[15] entitled 'Engineering Training for Industry'. The aim of this project is to develop a common method with a certain number of indicators and standards; to promote a Quality Charter for the training of engineers; to launch European evaluation of institutions and programmes and; to open negotiations with other international associations in this field (for example with ABET), on the basis of achieving mutual recognition. In the two cases mentioned, it is really a question of introducing a European label, to the extent that there is a common method used, common experts and the desire to satisfy employers by providing them with guarantees on quality, at a European level and therefore at an international level.

Conclusions

At the beginning of the twenty-first century, Europe, in terms of quality assurance, stands at a crossroads: which 'European dimension' are we going to work towards? Are those steps taken in the quest for quality assurance, at national level, by agencies and also by institutions themselves, going to result in the creation of a European evaluation agency or a European QA system, based on common criteria and taking into account new requirements stemming from Transnational Education? Is European accreditation, as introduced for business and engineering, going to extend to traditional disciplinary programmes and to all professional courses? Finally, are these two potential (and already more-or-less started) developments going to appear contradictory (the dynamic of accreditation running counter to the dominating culture in higher education systems) or are we going to succeed in achieving a degree of complementarity?

Moreover, we are facing these fundamental questions in a context that is continually evolving: will Europe be developed at several speeds (as is the case for the introduction of the Euro as a single monetary currency)? Will it move from a Union to a Confederation – with the next enlargement making it still more necessary to make major political decisions? Finally, what position is Europe going to take over the question of liberalising education, when negotiations are about to take place at the level of the World Trade Organisation, with the aim of integrating education into the sphere of services that can be commercialised?

Notes

1. Member States of the European Union are Germany, Austria, Belgium, Denmark, Spain, Finland, France, Greece, Ireland, Italy, Luxembourg, Netherlands, Portugal, United Kingdom, and Sweden. Otherwise the European Association of Free Trade includes Iceland, Norway and Switzerland.
2. Countries applying to join the European Union are Bulgaria, Cyprus, Estonia, Hungary, Latvia, Lithuania, Malta, Poland, the Czech Republic, Rumania, Slovakia, Slovenia, Turkey. On the website for the French Ministry of Foreign Affairs there is a good map of Europe: http://www.France.diplomatie.fr/europe/cartes/indexcarte.html
3. The Commission, the executive arm of the European Union, also has the right to introduce legislative initiatives.
4. There are 11 national languages in the European Union.
5. The European Report was written in two languages, English and French, and then translated into the other languages of the EU. It may be viewed in English on the Commission's website and in French on the site of the Comité National d'Evaluation, http://www.cne-evaluation.fr
6. *Evaluation of European Higher education: A Status Report*, prepared for the European Commission, DG XXII, September 1998. This report can be viewed on the website: http://www.enqa.net/
7. These *reviews* may be viewed on the CRE website: http://www.unige.ch/cre/activities/Quality/QA/CRE%20Reviews/Reviews/reviews_home.html
8. Council Recommendation, 24 September 1998, on European Cooperation in Quality Assurance in Higher education (98/561/EC). This Recommendation may be viewed at the following address: http://europa.eu.int/eur-lex/en/lif/dat/1998/en_398X0561.html
9. The Phare Programme is currently the main channel for the European Union's financial and technical cooperation with the countries of Central and Eastern Europe (CEECs), set up in 1989 to support economic and political transition.
10. Albania, Bulgaria, Czech Republic, Estonia, Macedonia, Hungary, Latvia, Lithuania, Poland, Romania, Slovakia, Slovenia.
11. Published in June 1998 by the European Training Foundation.
12. Published in November 1998 by the European Training Foundation.
13. http://www.enqa.net/.
14. The text of the Bologna Declaration is available on the CRE website: http://www.unige.ch/cre/activities/Bologna%20Forum/Bologna_welcome.htm, along with a range of documents pertaining to the European face of higher education.
15. Since 1995, there have been three principal European programmes, in the realm of education and professional training:

- Socrates, encouraging student mobility;
- Leonardo da Vinci, encouraging access to professional training;
- Youth for Europe III, encouraging the mobility of deprived young people.

Chapter Five

Academic Review in the United Kingdom

John Randall

Introduction

Higher education has changed fundamentally, from a system catering for a relatively small elite, to one based on mass participation. This chapter reflects on the consequences of this fundamental change for the assurance of quality and standards, against this background explains the establishment and functions of the United Kingdom's Quality Assurance Agency for Higher Education, and describes the new method of quality assurance known as *academic review*.

The Context

Academic standards are not a private matter. A substantial proportion of the population is now touched by higher education, as students, parents, employers and teachers. The transition of higher education from elite and exclusive, to mass and inclusive provision has transformed its relationship with the society that it serves. There are new stakeholders with expectations to be met and information needs to be satisfied: the greatly increased number of young people who are the first generation of their family to go to university, employers recruiting in the graduate labour market for the first time, and mature students looking to higher education to equip them with the skills to cope with uncertain and rapidly changing job prospects.

The public cares about academic standards. Employers, parents and young people committing three years of their lives to study need to have confidence that high standards are set by universities and colleges, and are achieved by their students. And all stakeholders wish to know how those standards relate to their needs for skilled staff, for successful careers, and for personal fulfilment.

In a small, elite university system, academic standards and values were implicit. Those who recruited graduates to blue-chip companies, to the professions and to public service were themselves graduates. Teachers in selective schools who advised their pupils where to study were a part of the same establishment. The value added by a higher education was well understood.

In an egalitarian, mass participation system, all that changes. Standards and values must be made explicit to those investing their time and money in study, and above all to those employers who will not know from personal experience of the value that higher education can add. Understanding of the benefits cannot be shared informally through a narrow social network, it must be widely available to all with an interest. As Lord Dearing put it in his report on higher education: 'there is much to be gained by greater explicitness and clarity about standards and the levels of achievement required for different awards'.

The transition to mass higher education is a global phenomenon. In both developed and developing countries higher education is expanding rapidly as governments identify high level technical and intellectual skills as being the key to success in knowledge based economies.

In most countries, universities find themselves subject to three pressures. First, there is the pressure to increase numbers of students. Second, governments find themselves unable to support financially a mass participation system at the rate per student that was affordable in a smaller, elite system. Third, universities are called upon to demonstrate that standards are being maintained and enhanced. The response to the pressures is similar in most countries.

First, there is a greater emphasis on the student as an active, and to an extent autonomous, learner, rather than a passive recipient of teaching. New learning strategies, including distance learning and the use of electronic materials, are developing from this change of emphasis.

Second, there is substantially increased participation of private finance in higher education. In some countries this manifests itself as a growth of private colleges operating as profit making enterprises. (Many UK universities franchise programmes to such institutions, notably in countries such as Malaysia.) In the United Kingdom private finance plays a part through the introduction of fees paid by students, and of public/private partnership approaches to some capital projects.

Third, many countries have established national organisations to provide an independent evaluation of quality and standards in higher education institutions. Initiatives to establish such bodies have come from governments, from within the higher education sector, or both. The International Network of Quality Assurance Agencies in Higher Education now has affiliates from some 50 countries throughout the world.

At the same time, the relationship between students and their teachers has altered as the student body has become larger, has grown to include more mature students and has become more representative of society at large. With all other professionals, university teachers are learning that deference to title or position has been replaced with respect for ability and quality of service. Public assurance of quality allows students and employers to make informed choices between institutions, and enables academics to earn that respect. Explaining what standards mean, and confirming that they are achieved by students, does no more than meet the proper expectations of transparency and accountability that a modern democracy has of those who provide it with professional services.

The Quality Assurance Agency

The Quality Assurance Agency for Higher Education was established in 1997 to provide an integrated quality assurance service for higher education institutions throughout the United Kingdom. Its establishment was recommended by a Joint Planning Group that was set up, with the approval of Government, by the higher education funding councils and the representative bodies of the institutions of higher education.

Higher education had become subject to three different forms of external scrutiny of academic provision. First, the universities themselves had established the Academic Audit Unit (later incorporated into the Higher Education Quality Council) in the late 1980s to report on the overall management of quality and standards by universities. Second, the Further and Higher Education Act 1992, which dissolved the Council for National Academic Awards, placed upon the Funding Councils a statutory responsibility to assess the quality of the provision that they funded. Each Funding Council established a quality assessment division to carry out reviews at subject level. Third, there were long-standing arrangements for accreditation of certain programmes by professional and statutory bodies for whom the programmes formed a part of the process leading to acquisition of a professional title. The Joint Planning Group recommended the establishment of a single Agency to integrate, as far as possible, these systems so as to achieve a greater efficiency and to minimize the burden of scrutiny on institutions.

In 1997 the National Committee of Inquiry into Higher Education, under the Chairmanship of Lord Dearing, made a number of specific recommendations about quality and standards. These have played a major part in setting the agenda of work for the Agency.

The Agency is an independent body, established as a company limited by guarantee and having charitable status. The members of the Company are the bodies representing higher education institutions, but the Board is structured so as to guarantee the independence of the Agency. Four members of the Board are nominated by the representative bodies, four are nominated by the Funding Councils, and six (of whom one must be the Chairman) are independent members appointed by the Board itself. The independent members are chosen so as to be broadly representative of employers of graduates. Two observers attend Board meetings, to represent the interests of students and of government education departments. The Agency inherited the staff and functions of the former Higher Education Quality Council, and of the Quality Assessment Division of the Higher Education Funding Council for England.

The Agency has two main funding streams. One comprises subscriptions paid by all institutions of higher education in the United Kingdom. The other is income derived from contracts with the Higher Education Funding Councils to carry out, on their behalf, reviews of provision at subject level to enable the Funding Councils to discharge their statutory responsibilities. The Agency contracts also with the Department of Health for the review of higher education programmes funded by that Department.

The Agency's mission is to promote public confidence that quality of provision and standards of awards in higher education are being safeguarded and enhanced.

The Agency reviews and reports upon the performance of over 180 universities and colleges of higher education. These institutions cover a wide range of activity, have varied backgrounds and operate in a climate of rapid change. The oldest is over 800 years old, whilst the newest was designated as a higher education institution in 2000. Student numbers at these institutions range from 120 to 200,000. Most institutions provide programmes in a number of subject areas. Others, such as art colleges or music schools, specialise in one area. The Agency also reviews the higher education programmes offered by some 270 further education colleges.

The Agency advises government on applications from higher education institutions for the grant of degree-awarding powers or university title. The Agency considers applications, normally over a complete annual cycle of academic activity, against criteria agreed between the Agency and government.

Additionally, in Scotland, the Agency advises on applications for designation as a higher education institution.

The Agency manages the scheme for recognition of Access to Higher Education courses. Access courses enable mature entrants to higher education, with non-traditional qualifications, to demonstrate an appropriate standard of attainment. Access courses are delivered by further education colleges but approved by Authorised Validating Agencies (AVAs), which are mainly consortia of higher education and further education partners. The Agency licenses the AVAs to make Access awards and use the official Access logo.

The Agency audits academic partnerships between UK institutions and overseas colleges that offer teaching leading to the award of degrees from those UK institutions. The purpose of the audit is to assess the effectiveness with which the UK institution is managing both the maintenance of standards of its awards made in respect of overseas programmes, and the quality of those programmes. This initiative enhances confidence in the work of UK universities and colleges operating overseas.

Reports of the Agency's findings are published. This information is helpful to prospective students, and their advisers, when applications are made to universities and colleges. It may be used also by employers who recruit graduates, and those professional and regulatory bodies, which recognise higher education awards that count towards their qualifications.

The provision of public information involves more than reporting on the performance of individual institutions. The key reference points against which the judgements in reports are made must also be available, understandable and understood. The Agency works with the higher education sector to define expectations about standards in an accessible manner.

For each main academic discipline subject benchmark statements are produced. These are statements that represent general expectations about standards for the award of qualifications at a given level in a particular subject area. Benchmarking is not about listing specific knowledge: that is a matter for institutions in designing individual programmes. It is about the conceptual framework that gives a discipline its coherence and identity; about the intellectual capability and understanding that should be developed through the study of the discipline to the level in question; the techniques and skills which are associated with developing understanding in the discipline; and the level of intellectual demand and challenge which is appropriate to study of the discipline to the level in question.

The Qualifications Framework is designed to ensure a consistent use of qualification titles so that there can be a clear understanding of the achievements and attributes represented by the main titles such as Bachelors degree with honours, Masters degree and doctorate. Through descriptors of typical outcomes, the framework helps students and employers understand the meaning and level of qualifications. It also provides public assurance that qualifications bearing similar titles represent similar levels of achievement.

The Agency publishes the *Code of Practice for the Assurance of Academic Quality and Standards in Higher Education*. This provides a point of reference for higher education institutions, by setting out precepts of good practice that should be addressed through internal quality assurance arrangements.

Academic Review

The Agency has developed a new quality assurance method known as *academic review*. It is being used for the first time in Scotland in the academic year 2000–01, and throughout the United Kingdom from 2001–02.

Academic review method seeks to assure quality by addressing three interdependent areas:

- reporting on *programme outcome standards* is concerned with the appropriateness of the intended learning outcomes set by the institution (in relation to relevant subject benchmark statements, qualification levels and the overall aims of the provision), the effectiveness of curricular content and assessment arrangements (in relation to the intended learning outcomes), and the achievements of students;
- reporting on the *quality of learning opportunities* in a subject is concerned with the effectiveness of teaching and of the learning opportunities provided; on the effectiveness of the use of learning resources (including human resources); and on the effectiveness of the academic support provided to students to enable them to progress within the programme;
- reporting on *institutional management of standards and quality* is concerned with the robustness and security of institutional systems relating to the awarding function. This involves, in particular, arrangements for dealing with approval and review of programmes, the management of credit and qualification arrangements and the management of assessment procedures.

Self-evaluation is central to, and is the starting point for the process of review. It encourages the institution to evaluate the quality of the learning opportunities offered to students, the standards achieved by them, and the effectiveness of arrangements to manage quality and standards. It provides an opportunity for the institution to reflect on 'what do we do?', 'why we do it' and 'why do we do it in the way that we do?'.

The reviewers who assess quality and standards are the peers of those whose work is under review. Peer review enables judgements to be made by those who understand the subject, the teaching and learning processes, or the academic management systems under scrutiny. It enables judgements to be credible to, and to command the respect of the academic community. It acts as a means of disseminating good practice. However, for a peer review process to have credibility with external stakeholders, such as employers and potential students, judgements must be made in a transparent manner and reported publicly; and the process itself must be seen to be accountable to a Board having a demonstrably independent membership.

Judgements on Standards

In each institution, and for each subject area, the Agency will make a single, threshold judgement about academic standards. Having regard to all of the matters listed below, reviewers will decide whether they have confidence in the academic standards of the provision under review. A 'confidence' judgement will be made if reviewers are satisfied both with current standards, and with the prospect of those standards being maintained into the future. If standards are acceptable, but there is doubt about the ability of the institution to maintain them into the future, reviewers will make a judgement of 'limited confidence'. If, in relation to any of the matters listed below, reviewers feel that standards are not being achieved, then their overall judgement will be that they do not have confidence in the academic standards of the provision under review.

Reviewers will assess, for each programme, whether there are clear learning outcomes that appropriately reflect applicable subject benchmark statements and the level of the award. Subject benchmark statements represent general expectations about standards in an academic discipline, particularly in relation to intellectual demand and challenge. The qualifications framework sets expectations for awards at a given level more generally. Reference points are thereby provided to assist reviewers in determining whether provision is meeting the standards expected by the academic community generally, for awards of a particular type and level. If the intended learning outcomes were found not to match those expectations, it is unlikely that reviewers could have confidence in the standards of the provision. An example of potential failure would be if a postgraduate programme had learning outcomes that were set at undergraduate level only.

Making consistent judgements about the appropriateness of the intended outcomes of academic programmes does not mean that reviewers will look for a dull uniformity rather than intellectual curiosity. Differing institutional aims within a plural sector will promote diversity. The Agency's *Code of Practice* has a section on programme approval which emphasises the importance of course design as a creative, and often innovative activity.

Reviewers will assess whether the content and design of the curriculum are effective in achieving the intended programme outcomes. It is the curriculum that ensures that students are able to meet the intended outcomes of the programme. Providers should be able to demonstrate how each outcome is supported by the curriculum. 'Curriculum' for this purpose includes both the content necessary to develop understanding and the acquisition of knowledge, and the opportunities to develop practical skills and abilities where these are stated as intended outcomes. If significant learning outcomes were found to be unsupported by the curriculum, it is unlikely that reviewers could have confidence in the standards of the provision.

Reviewers will assess whether the curriculum content is appropriate to each stage of the programme, and to the level of the award. Providers should be able to demonstrate how the design of the curriculum secures academic and intellectual progression by imposing increasing demands on the learner, over time, in terms of the acquisition of knowledge and skills, the capacity for conceptualisation, and increasing autonomy in learning.

Reviewers will assess whether assessment is designed appropriately to measure achievement of the intended outcomes. Providers should be able to demonstrate that achievement of intended outcomes is assessed, and that, in each case, the assessment method selected is appropriate to the nature of the intended outcome. There must also be confidence in the security and integrity of the assessment process, with appropriate involvement of external examiners. An assessment strategy should also have a formative function, providing students with prompt feedback, and assisting them in the development of their intellectual skills. There should be clear and appropriate criteria for different classes of performance, which have been communicated effectively to students. If significant learning outcomes appear not to be assessed, or if there are serious doubts about the integrity of the assessment procedures, it is unlikely that reviewers could have confidence in the standards of the provision.

Reviewers will assess whether student achievement matches the intended outcomes and level of the award. Reviewers will consider external examiners reports from the three years prior to the review, and will themselves sample student work.

Judgements on the Quality of Learning Opportunities

In each institution, and for each subject area, the Agency's judgements about the quality of the learning opportunities offered to students will be made against the broad aims of the provision and the intended learning outcomes of the programmes.

Reviewers will assess the effectiveness of *teaching and learning*, in relation to curriculum content and programme aims. They will consider large and small group teaching, practical sessions, directed individual learning, the integration of skills within curricula, and distance learning. Reviewers will evaluate the breadth, depth, pace and challenge of teaching; whether there is suitable variety of teaching methods; and the effectiveness of the teaching of subject knowledge; and of subject specific, transferable and practical skills.

Reviewers will evaluate *student progression* by considering recruitment, academic support, and progression within the programme. They will assess whether there is appropriate matching of the abilities of students recruited to the demands of programmes; and whether there are appropriate arrangements for induction and the identification of any special learning needs. They will assess the effectiveness of academic support to individuals, including tutorial arrangements and feedback on progress. They will consider general progression within programmes, and wastage rates.

In making judgements about *learning resources*, reviewers will consider how effectively these are utilised in support of the intended learning outcomes of the programmes under review. Consideration will be given to the use of equipment (including information technology), accommodation (including laboratories) and the library (including electronic resources). Reviewers will look for a strategic approach to the linkage of resources to programme objectives. Effective utilisation of academic, technical and administrative staff will be considered, as will the matching of the qualifications, experience and expertise of teaching staff to the requirements of the programmes.

Reporting on the quality of learning opportunities will place each of the three aspects of provision in to one of three categories, failing, approved or commendable, and will be made on the following basis:

- provision is failing because it makes a less than adequate contribution to

the achievement of the intended outcomes. Significant improvement is required urgently if the provision is to become at least adequate. In the summary report, this judgement will be referred to as '*failing*';
- provision enables the intended outcomes to be achieved, but improvement is needed to overcome weaknesses. In the summary report, this judgement will be referred to as '*approved*'. The summary will normally include a statement containing the phrase '*approved, but ...*', which will set out the areas where improvement is needed;
- provision contributes substantially to the achievement of the intended outcomes, with most elements demonstrating good practice. In the summary report, this judgement will be referred to as '*commendable*'.

Within the 'commendable' category, reviewers will identify any specific features of the aspect of provision that are exemplary. To be deemed '*exemplary*', a feature must:

- represent sector-leading best practice;
- be worthy of dissemination to, and emulation by, other providers of comparable programmes; and
- make a significant contribution to the success of the provision being assessed. Incidental or marginal features do not qualify for designation.

The characteristics of exemplary features will, by their nature, vary between institutions and programmes. The criteria listed above will ensure that features identified as 'exemplary' will be broadly comparable in weight and significance.

If provision is found to be failing in any aspect of quality, or if reviewers have no confidence in the standards achieved, the provision will be regarded, overall, as failing. It follows that all provision that is not failing is approved. The report of the review will state whether or not provision is approved.

Judgements on Institutional Management of Quality and Standards

Review by the Agency at the level of the whole institution is concerned particularly with the exercise by an institution of its powers as a body able to grant degrees and other awards. It results in reports on the degree of confidence that may reasonably be placed in an institution's effectiveness in managing the academic standards of its awards and the quality of its programmes.

Review will address the robustness and security of the systems supporting an institution's awarding function. In most cases, these will relate to the exercise of the institution's own powers. Where an institution does not have direct awarding powers, the review will consider the exercise of any powers delegated under a validation or other collaborative agreement. Review will be concerned with:

- procedures for approval, monitoring and review of academic programmes
- procedures for acting on the findings of external examiners, subject reviews, and other external scrutinies;
- the overall management of assessment processes;
- the overall management of any credit systems;
- the management of collaborative arrangements with other institutions.

If an institution has extensive partnerships, for example with further education colleges or overseas colleges, there may be a separate review of such collaborative activity to establish the extent to which an institution:

- is assuring the quality of programmes offered by a partner organisation for the institution's own awards; and
- is ensuring that the academic standards of its awards gained through study in partner organisations are the same as those applied within the institution itself.

Reports on whole institutions will be concerned with the effectiveness of an institution's systems for managing the quality of its provision, the standards of its awards and the security of its awarding function. The report will identify both good practice and matters where the Agency believes that improvement action should be taken. Action points will be categorised as essential, advisable or desirable on the following basis:

- *essential* – matters which are currently putting academic standards and/or quality at risk, and which require urgent corrective action;
- *advisable* – matters which have the potential to put academic standards and/or quality at risk, and which require either preventive, or less urgent corrective action;
- *desirable* – matters which have the potential to enhance quality and/or further secure academic standards.

Reports will conclude with a statement of the degree of confidence that the Agency considers may reasonably be placed in the continuing effectiveness of the institution's quality assurance arrangements.

A statement that confidence could not be placed in institutional quality assurance arrangements should be a rare occurrence. Such a statement would be likely to result from a number of matters requiring 'essential' action, the combined effect of which was to render ineffective the quality assurance arrangements as a whole.

A statement that limited confidence could be placed in institutional quality assurance systems would normally be made if there was one, or a small number of matters requiring 'essential' action, and it was clear that the failings could readily be put right. Such a statement might result also if there were no 'essential' action points, but a large number of matters where action was 'advisable'. The judgement would depend on the number, nature and weight of the 'advisable' action points.

In all other cases a statement will be made that broad confidence can be placed in institutional quality assurance systems. Use of the term 'broad confidence' ensures that an institution is not placed in a lower category on account of minor weaknesses only. The narrative of the report will discuss strengths and weaknesses, and may identify also exemplary features of the arrangements.

Conclusion

External evaluation of the quality and standards of higher education provision has three purposes. It must provide accountability for the public money and private resources invested in higher education. It must generate public information, especially about standards, that is useful and useable. It must promote enhancement of provision, through encouraging a reflective approach on the part of higher education teachers, and through the dissemination of good practice.

The new academic review method, developed in the United Kingdom, seeks to meet these needs through an emphasis on assuring the academic standards of the outcomes of higher education programmes.

References

'Higher Education in the Learning Society – Report of the National Committee of Inquiry into Higher Education' (The Dearing Report) (1997), HMSO.

Quality Assurance Agency (2000), *The Handbook for Academic Review*, London: Quality Assurance Agency.

Quality Assurance Agency (2001), *The Framework for Higher Education Qualifications in England Wales and Northern Ireland*, London: Quality Assurance Agency.

Subject benchmark statements, and sections of the Agency's *Code of Practice* are published on the Agency's website at www.qaa.ac.uk

Chapter Six

Quality Assurance of Higher Education in Denmark

Christian Thune
Danish Evaluation Institute (EVA)

Introductory Remarks

Denmark, like Hong Kong, is a small country. But Denmark, like Hong Kong also has strong ambitions that smallness shall be compensated by its higher education system being at the elite international level in terms of the quality of teaching and research.

The period of a formalised approach and framework for quality assurance in Denmark, however, is only a decade old. Danish Higher Education Institutions did not till the very late 1990s have any very strong tradition for giving a priority to quality assurance of teaching and learning. On the contrary especially the university level institutions were securely based in the Humboldtian idea of the university mission to be first and foremost research. Accordingly the search for established and operational internal systems of quality assurance in the universities would by 1992 have been a very futile one.

However, in 1992 the Danish government was one of the first countries in Europe to set up a national system for external evaluation of higher education. The Danish Centre for Quality Assurance and Evaluation of Higher Education (The Evaluation Centre) was established with the mandate to evaluate all higher education programmes at university and non-university level on a regular and systematic basis (Thune, 1994).

The establishment of the Evaluation Centre was a reflection of many and varied interests, trends and experiences. In the 1990s evaluation became a serious issue within educational policy. Evaluation came to be regarded as the natural consequence of parallel developmental trends in higher education, in Denmark as well as in many other European countries (Thune, 1997b).

The transition from elite education to mass education had changed the qualifications that students possess upon admission to higher education and called for ongoing quality assurance. At the same time national governments had concentrated more on monitoring the contents of higher educational programmes in connection with the allocation of resources. The desire to obtain 'value for money' was followed, in a number of countries, by a visible decentralisation process, where the state would withdraw and relinquish more and more of its competence and responsibility to the educational institutions themselves. ISO-9000 systems, TQM and other quality programmes from the private sector made their way into the public sector, including the education field. Finally, the internationalisation of students and studies had demanded international comparison at well-defined quality levels.

In Denmark these trends were linked to the joint efforts of the chairmen of the advisory bodies in higher education. The chairmen initiated from 1989 a series of pilot evaluations of higher education programmes and had encouraged the Minister of Education to set up an organisation to proceed with evaluations on a more formalised basis (Chairmen of the National Advisory Boards, 1992).

The Centre was set up for an initial period of seven years and on the condition that the Centre itself would be subject to an evaluation in order to decide whether it should become a permanent body. This evaluation took place in 1998 and a panel with international experts concluded in favour of the procedures and methodologies applied by the Centre (Thune and Kristoffersen, 1999).

The Centre had passed the test and could have been expected to continue on a permanent basis. The Centre did become central in a major new organisation of quality assurance of Danish education, but in the completely new context of the much more comprehensive Danish Evaluation Institute. This development will be treated in detail below after a brief presentation of the organisation of Danish higher education.

An Outline of the Nature of Higher Education Provision

In Denmark the system of higher education is administered centrally by the Ministry of Education's Department of Higher Education. Only certain programmes within such fields as art, architecture, librarianship and marine engineering are placed under other ministries (Danish Ministry of Education, 1996). The system is mainly financed by the State and the tuition is free of charge for the students.[1]

Higher education in Denmark is characterised by a binary structure, based on a separation of the non-university sector, i.e. the vocationally oriented programmes and the university sector. The non-university sector consists of mono-professional institutions, whereas the universities are poly-professional. The system is normally divided into two sectors: the non-university sector with short-cycle higher education and medium-cycle higher education; and the university sector with long-cycle higher education programmes, respectively. Each category will be further discussed below.

For a small country Denmark has succeeded in building up a remarkably complex and differentiated educational system. In higher education this is evidenced especially in the non-university sector where a large number of institutions offer study programmes of varying lengths and level: the short-cycle higher education area includes 70 institutions; the medium-cycle higher education area 112 institutions; and the long-cycle higher education institutions area includes 12 institutions. In addition, the Ministry of Cultural Affairs administers 21 schools, which are either medium-cycle or long-cycle higher education institutions.

The gross intake to higher education in general is of 56 per cent of those of a year group (Ministry of Education, 1999b, p. 21). They distribute with 9 per cent on the short-cycle, 38 per cent on the medium-cycle and 53 per cent on the long-cycle higher education programmes. Approximately 40 per cent of a year group finishes with a degree (Ministry of Education, 2000, p. 30). It is the stated government policy that 50 per cent of a year group obtains a higher education degree.

The size of the student intake is an institutional decision based on the available resources and the physical framework. The admission requirements are, however, set by the Ministry of Education. They are normally based on the examination result obtained at the end of upper secondary education, in some cases supplemented with points obtained from, for example, occupational experience.

The Non-university Sector

The short-cycle higher education programmes are most often of two years' duration. The sector covers a broad range of professional education within the technical, mercantile, scientific and agrarian areas. Education is closely tied to the labour market organisations that dominate programme committees and the school boards (Danish Ministry of Education, 2000b).

A new act concerning short-cycle higher education came into force on 1 July 1998. The short-cycle higher education programmes now presuppose either a vocational education or a general upper secondary education programme and have the common designation of 'vocational academy programmes'. Access to a short-cycle higher education has become broader and more transparent, with better possibilities for the students of being awarded credits if they continue to a medium-or long-cycle higher education programme.

Medium-cycle higher education programmes last typically between three and four years. Examples of medium-cycle higher education programmes are those leading to qualifications such as diploma engineer, librarian, teacher in primary school, journalist, social worker, nurse or physiotherapist. Both the short-cycle higher education sector and the medium-cycle higher education sector are characterised by a large geographical dispersal of their institutions.

In May 2000 the government agreed to reform the medium-cycle higher education and to establish the so-called 'Centres for Higher Education'.

A Centre for Higher Education is a self-governing body characterised by common/joint management and staff-community. It consists of several institutions, mainly providing medium-cycle higher education but in certain cases also short-cycle higher education, which have been merged. Geographically the merging institutions remain situated at their original locality and should maintain their own identity.

The stated objectives of the establishment of the centres are:

- to strengthen the non-university sector, through the establishment of educational environments oriented towards professions, which are big and broad enough to ensure coherent professional educational development;
- to maintain and strengthen the regional educational supply;
- a merger between various educational institutions will increase student and staff numbers and the programme supply, which in turn makes the institutions more competitive;
- to secure the continuation of strong educational environments outside the university sector proper.

These objectives were focused on solving two major problems: First, the proliferation of single profile institutions. For a country with 5 million inhabitants it must be termed impressive to muster 32 individual colleges for training of pedagogues primarily for the kindergarten and pre-school system. Second, the new centres could provide the framework for (minor) amounts of research funding thus reducing the distinction between medium and long-cycle higher education in terms of research based teaching and learning.

The universities had during the 1990s strongly opposed any government move to allow the medium cycle programmes to confer the BA. The main argument of the universities had been that the BA degree could only maintain its credibility if it was restricted to institutions with research. This argument suffered from the defect that the systematic programme evaluations of the Evaluation Centre had made evident that in many university programmes the majority of teachers at the undergraduate level were part time employed and without research opportunity. However, the government has accepted the stand of the universities and accordingly 2000 witnessed the birth of a new degree level that of a 'profession bachelor' for the medium cycle programmes. According to yet unclear criteria some of these but not all are in the coming year or two going to be allowed to offer this new degree.

The University Sector

Denmark has five multi-faculty universities and seven specialised university level institutions. The university institutions all offer Bachelor, Master and PhD programmes. The bachelor programmes are three-year programmes leading to a Bachelor's degree. The admission requirement for the Bachelor programmes is normally a qualification at general upper secondary level.

The bachelor programme constitutes in principle a complete programme in itself, but most students continue into a master's programme. When the government introduced the bachelor level in the late 1980s it met with total rejection by the universities. The government's arguments that the bachelor level would make study structures more flexible, ease internationalisation of Danish higher education, reduce dropout rates and create new types of job opportunities were met with a counter campaign over several years from the universities. The universities dismissed potential bachelors as half or less educated compared with masters and accordingly of no value to the job market. Media as well as employers accepted almost totally this rather conservative argument. The result has been that only a very small number of bachelors during the last couple of years have sought and got employment on the basis of this qualification.

Master programmes are of two years' duration and are normally a continuation of a Bachelor degree programme, i.e. a total of five years of studies. However, a few Master's programmes are still organised as one continual course without the Bachelor level. The designations of the research degrees proper are the PhD degree and the doctoral degree (dr. med., dr. phil., dr.scient. etc.), which is the highest academic degree (Danish Ministry of Education, 2000b).

The University Act of 1993

The study structure described above was consolidated through a new act for the universities and other research-based higher education institutions, that was introduced in 1993 (Danish Ministry of Education, 1997). The intention of the reform was to formulate the main objectives for and framework of the higher education sector and to give university level institutions the institutional freedom and autonomy to develop within this framework.

The reform was to ensure a tightening of each institution's management structure; to secure an undisturbed work environment; to find a better balance between supply of and demand for the institutions student capacity; and, finally, to improve the quality of the programmes, so that these came up to the highest international standards. Furthermore the act meant a massive authority transferral from the Ministry of Education to the higher education institutions; a preservation of the institutional democracy but a reduction of the number of governing bodies and their members; a significantly strengthened mandate and authority of rectors and deans; a separation of management of education and of research; and an external representation in the senate and faculty councils. A final cornerstone of the reform was the introduction of a new financing system, the so-called taximeter system, based on per capita grants (cash-per-student) to the institutions

Consequently, the key words of the reform were set out by the government to be deregulation and decentralisation, combined with mechanisms to ensure quality. The Minister of Education was to be responsible for the establishment of the framework for the obligatory admission requirements and the content of the different programmes, whereas the actual content of the individual programmes was to be drawn up by the institution itself – in curricula and study planning.

An important aim of the reform was that the changes caused by the reform and the pressure from a growing student population should not affect negatively the quality of programmes. Accordingly, a number of special provisions contributed to ensure continued educational quality and strengthening the central quality assurance through the Evaluation Centre and through reorganisation of the system of external examiners.

Higher education institutions were, from the outset, certainly sceptical towards the reform package. The criticism focused especially on the new uniform structure of studies and on the new University Act. The credibility of the intended process of decentralisation was also questioned, as was initially the new centrally based mechanisms for accountability of quality.

Specifically in the context of the stress on evaluations it could be said that on the one hand Government needed evaluations as a steering mechanism towards the modernised and decentralised field of higher education. The general development and trends of higher education should be monitored through evaluations, which simultaneously controlled the level of quality in individual programmes.

On the other hand the institutions of higher education received considerable real autonomy as a consequence of the new University Act. Accordingly the presidents, deans, and governing boards were now facing independent, broad and, often, difficult decision-making. Systematic evaluations would provide the institutions with an insight into the quality of their own study programmes. Good evaluations, which reflected the relation between institutional goals and realities, could therefore form the basis for planning and priorities of tasks. That at least was the ambition.

The Danish Centre for Quality Assurance and Evaluation of Higher Education

Accordingly in 1992 the Ministry of Education established the Danish Centre for Quality Assurance and Evaluation of Higher Education. The Centre was in principle an independent institution with respect to the Ministry of Education as well as of the Universities and other institutions of higher education. The Mandate of the Centre was:

- to initiate evaluation processes of higher education in Denmark including the university as well as non-university sector;
- to develop appropriate methods of assessing programmes;
- to inspire and guide the institutions of higher education in aspects concerning evaluation and quality;
- to compile national and international experience on evaluation of the educational system and quality development.

Accordingly a substantial part of the Centre's work consisted of regular and systematic evaluations of higher education programmes on a rotating basis in which almost all programmes were evaluated within a period of seven years.

In addition, the Centre for Quality Assurance and Evaluation of Higher Education evaluated new programmes after their establishment period, and programmes for which the Ministry of Education, consulting bodies or an institution of higher education found that there was a need for an evaluation of the quality of the programme.

Aims and Experiences of the Evaluation Centre

With regard to the actual task of evaluating and developing quality in higher education it was of decisive importance for the Evaluation Centre that the evaluations were based on a clear and well-defined foundation. In order to achieve this objective, however, it was necessary that the evaluations of individual educational programmes were systematic and transparent as well as founded on a well-defined concept. Thus a very important part of the Centre's work during the period 1992–99 was the development of consistent and comprehensive evaluation models and methods, in part based on cooperation with other European countries.

The basic Danish approach from the outset rested on a four-stage process:

1) the self-evaluation of the educational programmes based on a protocol presented by the Centre;
2) comprehensive surveys of the opinion on the quality of the programmes pronounced by users, i.e. students, graduates or employers;
3) site visits that were an important part of the total documentation analysed by the Centre and a panel of experts;
4) the publication of a report presenting an overall analysis of the quality of the programme field at the national level as well as individual analysis of the institutional level.

At the end of the function period of the Centre it became evident that a model had been developed which a considerable majority of Higher Education Institutions could accept and which could produce useful results. Instead of the concern and sensitivity that were at the outset shown towards external evaluations, the higher education institutions to an increasing extent rose to the challenge.

A number of explanations can be given for this development. First and foremost the Centre had been successful in establishing a suitable and workable division of labour between the professional staff of the Centre, the expert panel and the Higher Education Institutions. Other aspects worth mentioning are:

- a relevant balance between quality improvement and accountability;

- an ongoing contact and dialogue between the Centre and the higher education institutions;
- a compilation of comprehensive and trustworthy documentation for the evaluations;
- a point of departure in the evaluation process itself, without unnecessary dependence on pre-defined criteria for success or indicators of quality.

By 1999 the Centre had fulfilled its mission. The result was 62 evaluation reports some of which ran to 200 pages and covering almost all the programmes of both higher education sectors.

The Danish Evaluation Institute: Old Wine in a New Bottle

In May 1999, the Danish parliament passed a law proposed by government providing the legal background for a new institution – The Danish Evaluation Institute (EVA). One major inspiration for this governmental initiative was the relative success of external evaluation of teaching and learning in higher education. But probably more important was the intensifying political and media debate on the quality of the primary school system. The fuel for this debate was the relatively low Danish scores in international surveys of skills in reading and mathematics (Thune, 1999).

Accordingly the focus of this evaluation changed when the government launched the idea of establishing an evaluation agency not only responsible for the evaluation of higher education, but of all levels of the educational system from pre-schooling to Master's levels and including continuing and further education. The government decided to integrate the Centre into the Danish Evaluation Institute. In practical terms the implication was that the staff and experience of the former Centre formed the basis on which the new institute was launched.

By mid 2001 the Danish Evaluation Institute has grown to a staff of more than 50 and has presented its first major evaluations of various elements of the Danish educational system.

EVA's Organisational Structure

The Board governs the Institute; the board has 11 members and covers the main levels and sectors of education. The Minister of Education appoints board members, but the law is very elaborate in the paragraphs that provide the board with essential independence and integrity.

The Committee of Representatives comments on EVA's annual programme and the priority of planned activities. The Committee comprises 27 members appointed by the Board of the Institute, but on the recommendations of organisations of school proprietors, school associations, school boards and employers, rectors' conferences and school managers, social partners, teachers' organisations and student and pupil bodies.

EVA's Objective

EVA has two main tasks: to undertake on its own initiative systematic evaluations and to act as a national centre of knowledge, information and development in the field of educational evaluation. This dual purpose of the Institute is reflected in its organisational structure and in its annual programmes of action.

Each year EVA draws up a programme for the coming year's activities. The programme identifies the various projects to be initiated within the broad mandate set up by parliament.

In 2001 the section responsible for knowledge and information on evaluation will make a major survey on accreditation methodology and significantly strengthen the information and dissemination activities of the Institute.

In the evaluation section 10 major projects will be launched, including at the level of higher education evaluation of a university faculty, of programmes in information technology, and a pilot project on international evaluation covering the same programme in Denmark and two other European countries.

The major part of EVA's activities will be based on its own initiatives as presented in the annual programmes. However, EVA accepts also a number of contracts requested by the Ministry of Education, other ministries with educational responsibilities, or local authorities.

Evaluation Methods – Before and Now

At the time of the establishment of EVA, the evaluation methodologies were not specified. From the outset it was also stressed by the new institute that the aim was not a massive reproduction of the methodologies applied at the former Evaluation Centre. The Centre had applied a fairly standardised methodology thus ensuring that all study programmes were as far as possible treated in the same way, and making it possible to analyse and draw conclusions across the different evaluations.

EVA's broad mandate necessitates a move from standard methods to methodological pluralism in order that methods in any given project are relevant in the context of the educational segment under evaluation.

Evaluation methods vary, depending on the subject area. A given evaluation may involve the entire course of study, individual subjects, relationships between subjects/courses and a whole institution, relationships between Government or local authorities as owners on the one hand and colleges and institutions on the other hand. An evaluation, however, will always be based on the national and local objectives for the area in question.

However, the methodological lessons learned during the concentrated effort of the former Evaluation Centre are also a valuable inheritance for the new institute and may be recognised in the following list of elements normally included in EVA's evaluations:

- EVA conducts a *preliminary study* to each evaluation. It takes the form of a dialogue with all interested parties involved in the course of education and encompasses existing material relating to the field of education, e.g. regulations, government circulars, curricula, etc.;
- EVA drafts elaborate *terms of reference* for each evaluation, presenting objectives and a framework for the evaluation. The board of the Institute approves the terms of reference;
- the individual educational establishment conducts a *self-assessment*, presenting and analysing what it perceives as its own strengths and weaknesses;
- for each evaluation an *evaluation panel* is appointed. The members must have either a general or specific expertise in the field concerned;
- the evaluation panel *site visits* the educational establishments under review. The visit is planned in consultation with the individual establishments;
- in connection with each evaluation *user surveys* may be conducted among students, parents, graduates, employers or other groups;
- in its concluding and public report the evaluation panel presents its analysis, assessment and recommendations for developing the quality of the area of education in question.

The Dilemma of Purpose

EVA shares a principal dilemma with the former Evaluation Centre. This is the dilemma of purpose. The dilemma between an essential quality improvement related purpose and a purpose related to external accountability (Thune, 1997a).

In the 1998 evaluation report on the Centre it was one of the conclusions of the international panel that the Centre had in fact been able to combine the perspective of improvement and of accountability. In this respect EVA expects to follow closely in the footsteps of the former Centre. The result should be that in the Danish approach to evaluation the two perspectives of improvement and accountability are combined in terms of procedures, methods and goals in a dual approach with an emphasis on the improvement dimension. In the law of the Danish Evaluation Institute it is stated quite clearly in the first paragraph that the purpose of EVA is assurance and improvement of quality in higher education.

The Legacy of Best Practices from the Evaluation Centre

The credibility of evaluations is closely linked to the extent to which careful documentation is used to form the basis for conclusions and recommendations. The study programmes must be able to accept the basic evidence on which the conclusions and recommendations of the experts rest. Further the evaluation process, including the documentation, must inspire further and continuing internal quality assurance in the study programmes while at the same time there is a relevant basis for implementation of the evaluation.

To meet these aims the Centre had from the outset made a conscious effort to provide its own staff members with a clearly defined and broad responsibility for the evaluation. The *project leader* from the Centre was responsible for the whole process and the methodology, handled all contacts with the higher education institutions, prepared all internal and external meetings, and at the end drafted the final report. Probably the most distinct legacy from the Centre is therefore that the professionalism and size of staff is the crucial premise for a sequence of successful and consistent evaluations.

Another valuable experience is that the more the *self-assessment* is given priority in the process, the more the self assessment will function as training and preparing the institution or the study programme for taking over the responsibility for its own quality development – and the less the self-assessment is seen merely as producing information for the expert committee.

The self-assessment is the standard against which the institution can measure itself. It provides a framework for building up a definition of quality, it helps the institution decide how far it is achieving its strategic mission and goals, and it allows it to build an action plan for development.

In the qualitative context the self-assessment should be used to put more stress on inviting the study programmes to analyse their mission, values, goals and strengths and weaknesses respectively. Therefore the second and perhaps even more important purpose of the self-assessment is to provide the institution and the study programme with a commitment and a valid procedure and method to continue a process of quality assurance. It is very important to stress that the long term perspective of the effort vested in the self-assessments is less with delivering the material for a control process, but much more to contribute towards local quality improvement.

The members of the *expert panel* have the professional responsibility for the external part of an evaluation. Accordingly the selection process is crucial. The experts must possess a solid knowledge and understanding of the object of the evaluation while at the same time being independent of the programmes and institutions involved. In this context it is a well-known small state problem that it can be very difficult within the narrow confines of a small higher education system to find the necessary independent and unbiased experts. The Danish solution has been to recruit a large number of experts from the other Nordic countries. The Nordic experts have the necessary distance to their Danish colleagues and just as important they are able to read the documentation in Danish.

Another distinctive Danish practice has been to have a more open category of expert. In most other countries expert panels are comprised principally of 'peers', i.e. professional experts in the field concerned and with a background in university research. Danish practice has been instead to have expert panels consisting of both professional experts in the traditional sense and representation of the users or customers of higher education.

This practice reflects a general and long-standing Danish tradition for *focusing on users* in the planning of higher education. The attitudes of all three groups, the students, the recent graduates or the employers are surveyed intensively as part of the procedure of the individual evaluation. Furthermore representatives of employers are prominent in the evaluation panels.

The focus is not to deploy evaluation as a means of steering the higher education institutions more in the direction of the labour market. The dialogue between consumers and institutions should be balanced in such a way that the integrity and independence of the institutions are not in question. The role of the consumer is to give information and advice, not to take over the institutions,

Quality Assurance of Higher Education in Denmark 83

to dictate the content of education or to control the production. This balance is necessary, because the consumers do not have the knowledge and professional basis, on which education must be built. If the consumers took this role, there would be an obvious risk that education would be fit for the society of yesterday and not for the society of tomorrow.

The *evaluation reports* contain recommendations targeted at the higher education institutions themselves as well as at the Ministry of Education as the owner. In fact the majority of recommendations asks for implementation by the higher education institutions. The evaluation panels are instructed to focus on recommendations that are operational, constructive and realistic within the given conditions for the discipline area in question. Further, there should be a clear priority of recommendations, and preferably it should be evident which recommendations are essential in the short and which in the longer term. Finally it should be clear who must carry the responsibility for follow up or implementation.

The report is presented to the higher education institutions involved before publication. *A final conference* brings together all involved i.e. the expert panel, the project team and deans, course leaders and others from the study programmes evaluated. The latter have the opportunity for an open discussion with the former of the premises for the conclusions and recommendations of the report – which eventually may be redrafted in the light of points raised during the conference. The conferences as a rule produce very fruitful discussions and have a distinct potential as safety valves for the proceedings.

The follow-up procedure places the prime responsibility within the education institutions. Once an evaluation is finished the crucial phase of implementation of the conclusions and recommendations begins. As the aim of the evaluation process is the launching of a continuous process of quality assurance within the study programmes it is essential that the institutions themselves are committed to this follow-up. It is the firm belief of the Institute, however, that the institutions' incentive to initiate follow-up procedures are closely tied to the success of the self-assessment process and the openness of the self-assessment on the one hand and the operationality of the recommendations in the evaluation report on the other (Højbjerg and Kristoffersen, 1998).

The improvement perspective is certainly helped in two ways. Firstly the law on the Danish Evaluation Institute states explicitly that colleges and institutions must not be ranked in connection with the evaluations. Secondly there is no linkage between results of evaluations and funding of higher education. In many countries it is a much commented and controversial issue whether government's allocation of budgets to universities should wholly or in part be based on the results of systematic evaluations. In Denmark the fact that funding and evaluation have explicitly been de-linked has been a marked positive factor.

In some countries, where evaluation procedures have been established, the issue of *openness* has been controversial. The standard argument in favour of confidential proceedings has concerned the self-assessment. The argument runs that confidentiality should encourage the authors of the self-evaluation to be more honest and critical. In Denmark openness is viewed as a cardinal point with regard to the overall target of making evaluations the platform for qualified knowledge of the merits of various study programmes. All reports are therefore published or available.

The problem is of course the remarkable interest of the media and the politicians. Newsworthiness and political interest seem to be focused too much on the negative points of evaluation reports than on the more positive. EVA has set up its own information unit staffed by professionals. It is an important task of this unit to make sure that evaluations are presented to the public in a balanced manner that prevents the results from being misrepresented or misinterpreted.

The Role of the Institutions

After a period of initial scepticism towards quality assurance mechanisms and especially any external element the feedback from the institutions has over the last three or four years been increasingly affirmative. Two developments have acted as catalysts in this context.

First, the cycle of programme evaluations have had their effect and mostly positive. At the conferences during the final phase of the evaluation the institutional representatives have had their moment to speak their mind very freely in terms of their experiences of strengths and weaknesses of the process. Not least the experience of the self-assessment phase is generally considered in quite positive terms.

In connection with the external evaluation in 1998 of the Evaluation Centre itself a consultancy firm was commissioned by the Ministry of Education to do a so-called impact study of the evaluations of the Centre. This study mainly took the form of a large number of interviews with university presidents, deans and programme leaders. The majority of these gave evidence of support for and acceptance of the evaluations and the way in which these have been carried out even though the higher education institutions like to stress the fact that the self-evaluation process has taken up a large amount of human and financial resources at the institutions. The large majority of institutions have initiated follow-up activities but the extent of the follow-up depends of the area of evaluation. Accordingly, the evaluations have led to changes but most institutions interpret the reports as presentations of good advice and ideas and not as commands that must be obeyed.

University Performance Contracts

The other catalyst is the introduction in 1999 of University Performance Contracts as part of a reform of the Danish University Act from 1993. With this initiative contracts are now offered to the universities with the purpose of strengthening the development of institutional quality assurance in higher education. The primary aim of the reform is to 'put the main stress in governance on the individual university's goals and results' instead of on resource consumption, budgetary ties and general regulation. This would give each university the possibility of organising itself in accordance with its situation (Danish Ministry of Information, Technology and Research, 1999, p. 1).

A university performance contract is a declaration of intent between the university and the Ministry of Education. The contracts are intended to raise the universities' level of ambition, stimulate their inventiveness and improve their work in their core areas. They are based on a large degree of autonomy, with each university formulating its own standard and goals in a performance contract. Thus, the reform implies new values such as dialogue and agreement instead of control and top-down regulation.

Ten Danish universities have so far entered into agreement with the Ministry of Education (Danish Ministry of Information, Technology and Research 2000: 4). The number of goals and criteria in the individual contracts should be kept at a low level. In this way the contracts are clear and help to focus on the goals regarded as absolutely essential by the university and the ministry. The university and the ministry should further select a few key areas in which it is essential to set specific goals and include these in the contract.

The goals set up must be more than broad declarations. However, in those cases in which there are special and serious problems at an institution – indicated, for example, through an educational evaluation – the contract form could be used as the basis for more detailed agreements between the university and the ministry on how the problems in question are to be solved (Danish Ministry of Information, Technology and Research, 1999, pp. 8–9).

The overall focus of the 10 newly signed contracts is on developing the framework conditions that are a prerequisite for assuring the quality of research, teaching and other activities. Conditions such as organisational development and quality management mechanisms are thus of central importance. More specifically, the contracts reveal a diversity of goals, which reflect the different challenges and context of each university. Thus, the concrete goals set in the contracts vary greatly, with some universities adhering to overall goals and others to detailed and extended action plans.

This description fits even the various plans for increased internal quality assurance. Most universities have chosen rather vague declarations of future intentions that do not seem entirely credible in the light of past efforts in this direction. Not least in this context it is going to be interesting to see whether the Ministry of Education will try to evolve more consistent and transparent criteria for the follow up on the contracts.

Denmark in Europe and the World

During the 1990s systems of external evaluation of higher education have been established in almost all European countries. First the Evaluation Centre and now EVA have played a major role in advancing cooperation between national systems. These have despite their differences a common methodological core and have provided a focus on quality, transparency and accountability of higher education in Europe. An important step forward was the European Pilot Project; a large scale quality assurance exercise initiated by the EU commission and conducted in 1994–95 in 18 European countries. The Evaluation Centre in cooperation with the French agency, CNE, was responsible for the project and could in a later report conclude that the various national systems each had their individual character reflecting national tradition and culture of higher education, but at the same time they shared the same basic methodological approach. All national systems based thus their evaluations on self-evaluations, site visits by panels of experts and public reports (Thune and Staropoli, 1997).

However, the last few years have shown that there is a need for change and convergence of the systems of European quality assurance. The need for change is to a large extent related to internationalisation. The international changes affecting higher education are a growing international market for higher education, transactional education and a need for recognition of degrees due to graduate mobility (Campbell and van der Wende, 2000). The Bologna Declaration can be viewed as a European response to these developments. In relation to quality assurance all the countries, which have signed the Bologna Declaration of June 1999 commit themselves to 'the promotion of European cooperation in quality assurance with a view to developing comparable criteria and methodologies'.

In several European countries including Denmark a distinct debate has taken place after Bologna. The declaration is the expression of a serious attempt to harmonise the national systems of higher education. Briefly expressed the aim of the declaration is to stimulate a European system of further and higher education that in the terms of quality assurance solves the challenges of transparency, compatibility, flexibility, comparability, and protection.

The Bologna process has turned out thus to be a remarkable catalyst for a faster development in the European debate on internationalisation of higher education and quality assurance. Thus a number of investigations and mappings of this problem area is under way. One important framework is the established European Network of Quality Assurance (ENQA). The idea for ENQA was born out of the common experience of the European Pilot Project, which demonstrated the value of sharing and developing experience in the area of quality assurance across the member states of the Union and beyond (Enqa Newsletter 2000, p. 1). The idea was given momentum by the Recommendation of the Council of Ministers that followed publication of the Project's final report, and which has provided the opportunity for the Network venture to be brought to its present state. However, it is not least remarkable that European universities and especially their organisations have taken upon themselves a very active role in relation to the Bologna process. This active role is no doubt more than anything fuelled by the recognition of many universities that they are in a market place of higher education and that market value is linked to stamps of recognition, certification and accreditation.

The problem with the Bologna process, however, may well be that it propels the Danish and other European governments towards a common solution in formal terms for which there may be little basis in the realities of national strategies towards quality assurance. One of these realities may be linked to the remarkable growth in recent years in the fields of transnational education and of what is termed new means of delivery: distance education programmes, branch campuses, franchises and more.

The identification of relevant strategies is going to be a challenge in the near future. A list of possible scenarios could include:

- *national strategies* with an emphasis on regulation of importers or exporters of education;

- *international or regional strategies* based either on supra national quality assurance or on meta recognition of established national agencies;
- multi-*accreditation* implying either international recognition of national evaluation organisations and education structures or national recognition of a foreign organisation as accreditors.

One very important perspective for Denmark is that the existing well-established system of external quality assurance must now be reinterpreted in the light of the trend towards accreditation procedures. It is of course possible to argue that accreditation is a process that in methodological terms equals that of evaluations and quality assurance as practised by most European systems. However this misses the point that accreditation is basically a process based on clear and predefined standards or criteria and that at the end of the process a yes or no given to whether quality meets these standards. In that specific sense there has been in Denmark as in the other Nordic countries little previous experience.

In 1997 many ministers of education in Western European countries received a letter from the chairman of the National Committee on Foreign Medical Education and Accreditation in the US. The letter said that the medical programmes in these countries could not be recognised by the US because of a lack of an accreditation system. The Evaluation Centre drafted a reply to the Americans presenting the Danish evaluation system. The US reaction was a dismissal of the Danish efforts as not compatible with accreditation as understood in the US sense. The issue was eventually solved after more transatlantic exchanges. But the example illustrates that in the age of internationalisation of higher education the pressure on small countries such as Denmark and Hong Kong is strong to make their quality assurance systems visible and compatible in a wider regional and global context. Certainly this constitutes a major challenge for the Danes in the coming years.

Note

1 In 1996 the universities were formally transferred from the Ministry of Education to the Ministry of Research, but university education remained at the Ministry of Education. This division did not work well and in 2000 universities once became again the sole responsibility of the Ministry of Education.

References

Campbell, C. and M. van der Wende (2000), 'International Initiatives and Trends in Quality Assurance for European Higher Education, an Exploratory Trend Report', Helsinki: European Network for Quality Assurance.
Chairmen of the National Advisory Boards on Higher Education (1992), 'Quality assessment of Higher Education in Denmark', Copenhagen: Ministry of Education.
Danish Ministry of Education (1996), 'Higher Education', Copenhagen: Ministry of Education.
Danish Ministry of Education (1997), 'Higher Education in Principles and Issues in Education', Copenhagen: Ministry of Education.
Danish Ministry of Education (1998), 'Det 21. århundredes uddannelsesinstitutioner', Copenhagen: Ministry of Education.
Danish Ministry of Education (1999a), 'Regionale uddannelsesmønstre i Danmark', Copenhagen: Ministry of Education.
Danish Ministry of Education (1999b), 'UddannelsesRedegørelse 1999', Copenhagen: Ministry of Education.
Danish Ministry of Education (2000a), 'De videregående uddannelser i tal', Copenhagen: Ministry of Education.
Danish Ministry of Education (2000b), 'Higher Education in Facts and Figures. Education Indicators Denmark 2000', Copenhagen: Ministry of Education.
Danish Ministry of Education (2000c), 'Financing of Education in Denmark', Copenhagen: Ministry of Education.
Danish Ministry of Education and Research (1992), 'Education Reform – A Danish Open Market in Higher Education', Copenhagen: Ministry of Education and Research.
Danish Ministry of Information, Technology and Research (1999), 'University Performance Contracts for Denmark's universities', Copenhagen: Danish Ministry of Information, Technology and Research.
Danish Ministry of Information, Technology and Research (2000), 'University Performance Contracts – The Danish Model', Copenhagen: Danish Ministry of Information, Technology and Research.
Enqa Newsletter (2000), No. 1, June, Helsinki: The European Network for Quality Assurance.
The Evaluation Centre (1997), Report of Activities 1992–1997, Copenhagen.
Højberg E. and D. Kristoffersen, (1998), 'Denmark', in Jacob Scheele et al. (eds), *To be Continued ... Follow-up of Quality Assurance in Higher Education*, Amsterdam: Elsevier.
Thune, C. (1994), 'Setting up the Danish Centre', in A. Craft (ed.), *International Developments in Assuring Quality in Higher Education*, London: The Falmer Press.Thune, C. (1999),
Thune, C. (1997a), 'The Balance Between Accountability and Improvement: The Danish Experience', in John Brennan et al. (eds), *Standards and Quality in Higher Education*, London: Jessica Kingsley Publishers, pp. 87–103.
Thune, C. (1997b), 'The European Systems of Quality Assurance – Dimensions of Harmonization and Differentiation', paper presented at the International Dissemination Conference on Quality Assessment in Higher Education (OECD/IMHE), 1–2 December, Mexico City.
Thune, C. (1999), 'Denmark Launches a Single Organisation for the Evaluation of all Levels of Education', Accreditation Newsletter August 1999, Hong Kong: HKCAA.
Thune, C. and D. Kristoffersen (1999), 'Guarding the Guardian: The Evaluation of the Danish Centre for Quality Assurance and Evaluation of Higher Education', paper presented at the 5th Biennial Conference of Evaluation of Higher Education, May, Santiago, Chile.

Thune, C. and A. Staropoli, (1997) 'The European Pilot Project for Evaluating Quality in Higher Education', in Brennan et al., op. cit., pp. 198–204.

Chapter Seven

Accreditation and Quality in the United States: Practice and Pressures

Judith S. Eaton
Council for Higher Education Accreditation, USA

In the United States, accreditation is the primary form of external quality review of colleges, universities and programmes. Accreditation is carried out by private non-profit organisations designed for this specific purpose and is a non-governmental enterprise. It is more than 100 years old, emerging from concerns to protect public health and safety and to serve the public interest.

The use of the term 'accreditation' is the US is not identical to how the term is used in other countries. An institution or programme is considered accredited if it 1) meets the standards of an accrediting organisation, 2) sustains effective means of assuring quality – has processes and mechanisms to manage quality and 3) maintains strategies to improve its quality over time. Accreditation involves compliance with quality standards, mechanisms for quality assurance and strategies for quality improvement.

Accredited status does not give an institution or programme a license to operate. Authority to operate is granted by individual states in the US, not by accreditors. Accreditation does not guarantee transfer of credits between two accredited institutions and it does not guarantee degree equivalency among accredited institutions. Determination of transfer and degree equivalence are the province of individual institutions and programmes, not accreditors.

The US accreditation structure is decentralised and complex, mirroring the decentralisation and complexity of American higher education. Approximately 6,500 degree-granting and non-degree-granting institutions that may be public or private, two- or four-year, non-profit or for-profit were accredited in 1998–99. More than 20,000 programmes in a range of professions and specialties that include law, medicine, business, nursing, social work and pharmacy, arts and journalism were accredited in 1998–99 as well. The US higher education enterprise spends approximately $230 billion per year, enrols more than 15 million credit students and employs approximately 2.7 million full- and part-time people.

Regional organisations accredit public and private two- and four-year institutions. Almost all of these colleges and universities are non-profit and degree-granting. Regional accreditors undertake a comprehensive review of all institutional functions. They are called 'regional' because, historically, this institutional accreditation in the US has been organised in clusters of states or regions of the country, with the scope of these particular accreditors limited to these states.

National organisations accredit public and private two- and four- year colleges and universities as well. Some national organisations focus on faith-based or other single-purpose institutions. Others review primarily for-profit degree-granting and non-degree-granting institutions. Yet others review a combination of for-profit and non-profit institutions. They are called 'national' because their scope includes all 50 states and, unlike regional accreditors, they are not confined to certain areas of the country.

Specialised and professional organisations accredit specific programmes or schools including law schools, medical schools, engineering schools and programmes and health profession programmes. They are called 'specialised and professional' because their scope is confined to specific educational areas rather than entire institutions.

The Purposes of US Accreditation

US accreditation serves several purposes. These are to:

1) Indicate quality

Accredited status is a signal to students and the public that an institution or programme meets at least minimal standards for e.g., faculty, curriculum, student services and libraries. Accredited status is conveyed only if institutions and programmes provide evidence of fiscal stability as well.

2) Assist with access to US federal funds

Accreditation is required for access to US federal funds such as student grants and loans for tuition and other federal programmes. The federal government relies on accreditors to confirm the quality of institutions and programmes in which students enrol. Federal student aid funds are available to students only if the institution they are attending or the programme in which they are enrolled is accredited by an organisation 'recognised' by the United States Department of Education (USDE), a federal agency. (Please see below, 'Holding Accreditors Accountable'.) The United States awarded $60 billion in student grants and loans in 1997–98.

3) Ease transfer

Students who wish to move from one institution to another and have their credits transfer must have these credits scrutinised by the receiving institution or programme to which they want to transfer. These institutions and programmes examine, among other things, whether or not the credits a student wishes to transfer have been earned at an institution or programme that is accredited. Although accreditation does not guarantee transfer and is but one among several factors taken into account by receiving institutions, it is viewed carefully and is considered an important indicator of quality.

4) Engender employer confidence

Employers consider accredited status of an institution or programme when evaluating credentials of job applicants and when deciding whether to support tuition requests from current employees seeking additional education.

Accredited status is not a requirement in the US, but is highly coveted because of the purposes that it serves.

How Accreditation Operates

Review of institutions and programmes for US accredited status may occur every few years to every 10 years. The earning of accreditation is not a 'one-time' event. Periodic review is a requirement for all US institutions and programmes to remain accredited.

To obtain accreditation, an institution or programme must go through a number of steps stipulated by an accrediting organisation. These steps include preparation of evidence of the activities and accomplishments of the institution or programme, scrutiny of this evidence and a site visit by faculty and administrative peers and action to decide the accreditation status of an institution or programme.

More specifically, accreditation has five key features:

- *institutional or programme self-study*: institutions and programmes prepare a written summary of their performance based on an accrediting organisation's standards;
- *use of peer review*: faculty and administrative peers review the self-study and serve on visiting teams that examine institutions and programmes after the self-study is completed. Peers also serve on accrediting commissions or boards that make judgements about whether the institution or programme is to be accredited;
- *reliance on site visit*: a visiting team is usually dispatched by an accrediting organisation to review an institution or programme. The self-study is the basis for the team visit. Peers, accompanied by public members (non-academics who have an interest in higher education), generally make up the team. All team members are volunteers and are usually not compensated. Some accreditors do provide may a modest stipend for service;
- *accreditation action (judgement)*: accrediting commissions make judgements about whether institutions and programmes will receive accreditation or whether accreditation will be denied;
- *periodic external review*: institutions and programmes continue to be reviewed in cycles of every few years to 10 years. A self-study and site visit are usually part of this periodic review.

Accreditation organisations and their activities are primarily funded by US colleges and universities and programmes themselves. These institutions and programmes pay the cost of the accreditation review and annual membership dues to accrediting organisations. Some accreditors have grants for foundations or corporations, but these funds are not primary sources of ongoing revenue.

Holding Accreditors Accountable

In the US, accreditors are accountable to the institutions and programme they accredit. They are also accountable to the public and government. To address the accountability demands of these constituents, accreditors undergo a periodic external review of their organisations known as 'recognition'. Recognition of an accrediting organisation is based on specific standards. The scrutiny culminates in a judgement about whether the accreditor has met the standards.

Accreditation and Quality in the United States: Practice and Pressures   95

Recognition is carried out either by another private organisation, the Council for Higher Education Accreditation (CHEA), a national coordinating body for national, regional and specialised accreditation or, as indicated above, the USDE, a US federal agency. Approximately 75 institutional and programmatic accreditors are currently recognised by either CHEA or the USDE. Although accreditation is a non-governmental activity, recognition may or may not be.

The five recognition standards used by CHEA to review accrediting organisations place primary emphasis on academic quality assurance and improvement for an institution or programme. These standards require accreditors to advance academic quality, demonstrate accountability, encourage purposeful change and needed improvement, employ appropriate and fair procedures in decision-making and continually reassess accreditation practices.

CHEA recognition calls for review at least every 10 years with a five-year interim report. The CHEA Committee on Recognition (a group of institutional representatives, accreditors and public members) reviews accreditors for CHEA recognition based on a self-study completed by the accreditor. CHEA may also conduct a site visit. The committee recommends to the CHEA governing board that recognition be affirmed or denied to an accreditor. The CHEA board determines whether or not an accreditor is recognised.

The USDE recognition review usually takes place every five years. USDE review involves a written petition from the accreditor and, at times, a visit to the accreditor. USDE staff recommend to the National Advisory Committee on Institutional Quality and Integrity (NACIQI). This is a group of educators and public members appointed by the US Secretary of Education and charged to recommend the recognition or denial of recognition of an accrediting organisation. The committee, in turn, recommends action to the US Secretary of Education. The Secretary determines whether or not an accreditor is recognised.

There are 11 USDE standards for recognition in federal law. They address the multiple dimensions of institutional or programme operation, including student achievement, curriculum, faculty, libraries, student affairs, finance, governance, continuing education, facilities and recruitment and admissions. The fundamental thrust of the federal review is to assure that the resources and capacity of an institution or programme are highly likely to produce student achievement.

CHEA and USDE recognise many of the same accrediting organisations, but not all. Accreditors seek CHEA or USDE recognition for different reasons. CHEA recognition confers an academic legitimacy on accrediting organisations, helping to consolidate the place of these organisations and their institutions and programmes in the national higher education community. USDE recognition is essential for accreditors whose institutions or programmes seek eligibility for federal student aid and other federal funds.

Recent Challenges: Pressures on US Accreditation

Accreditation in the US finds itself beset by a number of pressures. Some of these pressures are not unique to the US and may be found in a number of other countries. Some reflect specifically US issues and concerns about quality review:

- pressure for accreditation to become more public with its reviews and decision-making;
- pressure to provide more information about student learning outcomes in addition to information about resources and processes of institutions and programmes;
- pressure to accommodate more and more electronically-delivered degrees, programmes and courses in addition to scrutiny of site-based activity;
- pressure to act internationally as well as nationally;
- pressure to act nationally in addition to operating regionally (in the case of the regional accreditors).

These pressures on accreditation have the potential to reposition the role of accreditation in US society. Accreditation would shift from a primarily private undertaking that directly serves college and universities in their efforts to assure and improve quality to a more public undertaking that directly serves students, the public and government through providing consumer and market information about quality, especially student learning outcomes.

Historically, accreditation has been a system of self-review intended to improve the capacity and resources of institutions to undertake teaching, learning and research. It is a catalyst for creating an ongoing institutional conversation about the management of quality. Accreditation has been driven by traditional academic values (e.g., the values of institutional autonomy, academic freedom and general education) with institutions as the primary audience of accrediting efforts. Accreditation has been a powerful force for continuity in US higher education.

Increasingly, however, accreditation is expected to take on additional and, in some ways, quite divergent tasks. These tasks include providing detailed public information about the results of accreditation review, with particular attention to student learning outcomes. Accreditors are asked to pay specific attention to student information needs and public and government concerns about quality for money. This contrasts with the heretofore private role of accreditation review and with the primary focus of accreditation review on institutional capacity and resources, rather than outcomes.

For example, accreditors are increasingly asked to provide consumer protection, shielding students from poor quality higher education by making public information about marginal or inadequate institutions, whether they are accredited or not. Students want to know about 'diploma mills' and 'accreditation mills.' Accreditation is also becoming an indicator of the market value of a higher education programme or institution. For example, corporations moving into higher education seek accreditation more because it enhances the worth of their investment to the public and less because it is instructive about managing quality.

Finally, in this repositioning, accreditation is supposed to be a significant force for change (in contrast to a force for continuity) – accommodating the growing diversity of new providers and student attendance patterns in higher education by functioning as the arbiter of quality and providing a basis for public judgements about these new providers and patterns. The expectation is that e.g., distance learning operations, the growing for-profit sector in higher education and more and more programmes that involve course-taking not leading to a degree – all will be scrutinised for quality by the accrediting community. Little attention is paid to the extent to which these new providers are significantly at variance with the type of higher education institutions and programmes that accreditation was invented to assist.

Pressure on All US Accreditors to Make Reviews and Decisions More Public

As indicated above, US accreditation is a private activity – carried out by non-governmental bodies. In addition to this private status of the organisation itself, the accreditation review and decision-making process is similarly private. Especially in the private higher education sector, institutional self-studies and team reports are not likely to be public documents. For both public and private institutions, accrediting commission deliberations about accredited status are not public. Accrediting organisations are required only to provide public information about their ultimate decisions regarding the accredited status of colleges and universities.

The rationale for this privacy is that accreditation review is intended as a formative evaluation that takes place among peers. To make this evaluation public would reduce the likelihood of candid exchange among peers, thereby reducing the consultative value of the accreditation review to improve the quality of performance of institutions. Although a number of countries routinely make this review public, the US does not.

Nonetheless, as higher education becomes both an increasingly essential and expensive commodity in the US, constituencies such as federal and state governments, students and the general public want to know more about what goes into the ultimate decision about accredited status. Why does one institution become accredited and another is denied accreditation? Why do few institutions lose their accredited status?

These same constituents are also calling for additional evidence on which to make comparative judgements about institutional and programmatic quality. Ranking systems – publications such as *US News and World Report's America's Best Colleges, Yahoo* and *The Princeton Review* – are quite popular and have emerged as a significant source of information to students and the public about higher education and comparative quality. Ranking systems are sometimes juxtaposed to accreditation as evidence that these constituents want ways to make comparisons between and among higher education institutions and that accreditors should provide this information.

Such comparative judgements are neither easy nor, for a number of accreditors, desirable. The confidentiality of a review's detailed results creates hurdles for comparative judgements about quality. Accreditation relies on the mission of an institution or programme as the key basis for judgement about its quality. This, too, makes comparative judgement difficult. For example, an accreditation standard about curriculum is the same for a community college and a research university. At the same time, what counts as evidence of meeting this standard effectively is expected to vary considerably, based on the distinct missions of these two types of institutions. How can meaningful and reliable comparisons be made?

This pressure for more information about the accreditation review is, at its core, an growing interest in institutional and programme quality. One way that accreditors can respond is to work through the institutions and programmes they accredit so that these operations provide more public information about quality. Accreditors can hold institutions and programmes accountable for expanded information-sharing practices as one way to respond to this pressure.

This information can be obtained through, for example, electronic institutional and programmatic portfolios or 'fact books' describing performance. Accreditors might also urge that institutions and programmes develop a 'quality grid' based on data that describe the effectiveness of the institution or programme. This grid or matrix of quality would contain information about, e.g., the likelihood of graduation or the achievement of other educational goals, certification or licensure success, and rates of transfer and employment all help students to make decisions about college attendance. The grid could include data on documented student competencies. Institutions and programmes might also consider developing a 'performance profile' – information to the public about annual goals and provide evidence that these have been achieved.

Pressure to Become More Outcomes Focused

In addition to the public interest in a more public accreditation review, constituents are also seeking more information about student learning outcomes. These constituents ask: what are the student learning outcomes associated with a college, university or programme? What counts as evidence of student learning outcomes? How does this evidence contribute to our judgements about institution or programme quality? Accreditors are asked to inform students and the public about the learning gains and competencies of students in response to the oft-repeated query: is this a quality institution or programme?

In response, accreditors have begun to cast their standards and their expectations of institutional and programmatic performance in terms of 'outcomes' or what student learn. They are building capacity to work with institutions and programmes to develop evidence of student learning and assisting the institutions and programmes themselves to develop capacity to do this. However, there is great resistance within the higher education community to moving toward student learning outcomes as a means to manage quality.

Some institutions and programmes claim they already have evidence of student achievement or learning outcomes (grades) and do not understand why other constituents of accreditation state that this information is not available. They maintain that faculty in the classroom have good evidence of student learning outcomes and should not be pressured to provide more. These institutions and programmes further maintain that recent pressure for additional attention to student learning outcomes is a call to reduce the teaching and learning experience to only measurable objectives that does not capture the fullness of the collegiate experience.

Although the current evidence of student learning outcomes may satisfy some in higher education, it is simply not enough for accreditation's other constituents outside colleges and universities. This helps to explain why some states in the US have begun to require that public colleges and universities to provide such evidence as a condition of obtaining state public funds. It also clarifies why the US Congress and the USDE, in the 1998 reauthorisation of the federal Higher Education Act (HEA), chose to place additional emphasis on student achievement as a determinant of quality. The HEA is the federal legislation governing federal funds to higher education. HEA also addresses accreditation and a number of other higher education issues.

While acknowledging that institutions and programmes do make some judgements about student learning outcomes, accreditors can nonetheless work with institutions to develop additional capacity to respond to this pressure. This might include obtaining direct evidence of student competencies through tests, portfolios or other means in addition to grades. Accreditors can hold institutions and programmes accountable for developing and using evidence of student learning outcomes to make judgements about institutional and programmatic quality and how to improve it. Some institutions have been successful in this area, and some accreditors have been discussing the feasibility of urging others to approach student learning outcomes in this way.

There are some models available. CHEA has developed a *Competency Standards Project*, an alternative accreditation review based on student learning outcomes. The standards for the review focus on student achievement, institutional support for student achievement and institutional organisation for student achievement. It is available through CHEA, with an overview on the CHEA website (www.chea.org). Corporate information technology training from, for example, Microsoft or Cisco, is built on a competency model, offering higher education a way of organising a determination of quality through attention to outcomes. An estimated 2.4 million information technology certifications were issued worldwide in 1999.

Pressure to Address the Expanding World of Electronically-delivered Education

With the growing numbers of students, traditional institutions and new providers of higher education engaged in electronic delivery of higher education; accreditors are being asked to build capacity to assure quality in these environments. Institutions and programmes want to assure that their emerging electronic initiatives are sustaining quality; students and the public want to know which of the many electronic initiatives are worthy of tuition dollars and time; federal and state governments want to make sure that any use of public tax dollars is confined to quality higher education operations.

Electronically-delivered education takes several forms. First, traditional site-based institutions and programmes are incorporating electronic delivery into existing courses and programmes or establishing on-line colleges. Some are developing entire degrees. University of Maryland University College (UMUC), for example, enrolled 40,000 students in 1999–2000 in on-line programmes. Second, electronically-based consortia of courses, programme or institutions are developing. For example, the Southern Regional Education Board (SREB) has developed an electronic campus with more than 3,200 on-line courses and available through more than 260 institutions in 16 states in 1999. Third, 'new providers' of higher education that rely primarily on electronic delivery are emerging. Virtual universities such as United States Open University and Western Governors University are two examples.

Whatever the form of electronically-delivered education, it creates responsibilities for accreditors. Working with institutions and programmes, they are responsible for identifying the distinctive features of distance delivery and assuring that quality review practices are adequate to review these features. This could include reconsideration of existing accreditation standards or the development of new standards. Especially in the case of virtual universities, this may involve greater attention to student learning outcomes that in a site-based setting.

Accreditors, institutions and programmes also have political responsibilities, working to demonstrate to the federal government that their quality review practices that have been effective for site-based education can be equally effective when applied to electronically-based environments. They have responsibility for working with government to rethink the federal student grant and loan programmes where electronic delivery alters existing policy agreements.

The eight US regional accreditors have responded to this pressure with the development of a common platform of inquiry and scrutiny of distance-delivered education. The are currently reviewing a proposed set of practices for the review of electronically-offered degree and certificate programmes. While each of the regional accreditors will continue to rely on the specific quality standards of their respective regions, the set of practices provide a common foundation for application of these standards to distance delivery.

Some of the national and specialised accreditors have developed specific quality standards for distance delivery. Other accreditors are continuing to use existing standards, but are developing additional strategies to accommodate some of the variations in teaching and learning that especially computer-mediated instruction has introduced. For example, AACSB – The International Association for Management Education – has identified key issues in distance learning while the National Council for Accreditation of Teacher Education has published key questions about distance learning and teaching education.

Pressure to Act Internationally

Pressure on accreditors to expand their international review activity is increasing. There is a growing interest in US institutions and programmes to operate internationally and a growing interest of accreditors in undertaking more and more reviews of non-US-based institutions and programmes. The US federal government is giving greater attention to international higher education. Institutions and programmes around the world are coming to value of the US accreditors' seal of approval and more and more are approaching them for review. And distance-learning operations can very quickly go international, which calls for additional attention to this area.

In addition, with distance learning enabling students to wander the globe in search of educational experiences and distance providers free to beam their wares anywhere, accreditation and quality assurance agencies and organisations are finding themselves besieged with requests for judgements about institutions throughout the world. Students in one country, for example, want information ranging from transfer of credits to admission to graduate school to tuition reimbursement to the portability of degrees across the globe. These questions simply cannot be answered without attention to fundamental quality issues.

At present, accreditation of US institutions and programmes operating outside the US or of non-US institutions and programmes operating outside the US is fairly limited. In 1999, the 56 CHEA participating accreditors reported that they were accrediting 355 institutions or programmes, almost all of which are US institutions operating outside the US These US accreditors, along with their international colleagues, are energetically seeking alliances with quality assurance agencies to obtain more and better information about the operation and quality of institutions and programmes in other countries. In addition, they are exploring avenues such as substantial equivalency, mutual recognition, meta-accreditation and transfer networks.

Accreditation and Quality in the United States: Practice and Pressures   103

These international challenges before US accreditors include examining whether, at some point, they need to coordinate standards for international quality review among institutional and programmatic reviewers. Perhaps even more pressing for the US is the need to examine the terms and conditions under which US accreditors are individually willing to undertake an international review. Some accreditors review US institutions and programmes operating abroad; others do not. Some accreditors review non-US institutions and programmes operating outside the US; others will not. Should there be more coordination here? Or, as long as each accreditor is clear about its willingness to operate internationally, is the current situation satisfactory? Finally, there is a need to expand communication and cooperation between US accreditors and quality-assurance organisations around the world.

Pressure on Regional Accreditors to Act Nationally

As mentioned above, there are eight regional accrediting commissions in the US, each accrediting institutions in a specific cluster of states. Distance learning institutions (e.g., Western Governors University) and site-based institutions operating cross-regionally (e.g., University of Phoenix) have called into question whether the long-standing regional structure should give way to a national approach to accreditation. For some, emerging distance learning offerings and site-based institutions operating cross-regionally render a strictly regional approach obsolete. This 'acting nationally' might take place through regional commissions adopting a set of national standards to which all eight commissions subscribe to make judgements about institutional quality. The commissions would exist to apply the national standards.

However, the response of the regional commissions to 'nationalise' in this way has been an emphatic 'no'. They – and their institutional constituents – are powerfully committed to retain a regional structure with regional standards. To accommodate this, the regional commissions have taken two steps. First, they have all approved a common policy for the accreditation of site-based institutions operating cross regionally. Regional standards prevail, but the conduct of an accreditation review involves consultation and decision-making among regions in which the institution is operating.

Second, as mentioned above, the regional accreditors have developed a draft common platform for review of distance learning to respond to the pressure of expanded electronic delivery. This platform is also a response to the pressure to nationalise. The platform does stipulate common areas of inquiry that the regional commission should pursue such as institutional context, curriculum, faculty, student support and evaluation. It does not, however, impinge on specific regional accreditation standards and judgements about quality made by a region. These standards and judgements are the sole province of the regional accrediting organisation.

The five pressures on accreditation in the US have the potential of fundamentally altering accreditation activity. The more likely outcome, however, is something more modest than fundamental change. Accreditation will be modified in some ways – perhaps greater emphasis on student learning outcomes, some additional attention to public information and more accommodation of electronic delivery. At the same time, the basic commitments of accreditation will remain: the commitment to peer review, a consultative style and primary emphasis on quality improvement.

Summary

Accreditation in the US is a complex set of activities involving dozens of accrediting organisations and thousands of institutions and programmes. Accreditation involves compliance with accreditation standards as well as capacity for quality assurance and quality improvement. While not required for institutions and programmes, it is a coveted status because it brings the benefits of access to government funding, strengthening employer confidence in education and easing transfer of credit (in addition to assuring quality).

Accreditation is also the primary means by which US colleges and universities sustain their institutional autonomy and self-regulating authority. It is a peer-driven, consultative process culminating in a judgement about whether or not an institution or programme is may be designated as accredited.

At present, there are five major pressures on accreditation. Accreditation is being pushed to become more public, to provide more information about student learning outcomes, to accommodate more electronically-delivered education, to increase international activity, and (for regional accreditors) to operate nationally. The fundamental challenge for accreditors is to respond to these challenges while maintaining the desired traditional features of their enterprise. For some of these pressures, this appears promising. For other pressures, it is more difficult.

Underlying these pressures are various forces that would reposition accreditation in the US from a primarily private activity intended to serve the quality assurance and improvement needs of colleges and universities to a more public activity to serve the needs of consumers, the market and government in making judgements about quality for the purposes of decision making about what college to attend, business investment in higher education and use of taxpayer dollars for tuition.

Whatever the pressures, accreditation in the US will remain a powerful and important presence in higher education, to government and to the public. The accrediting community's response to these pressures and what underlies them will determine whether and to what extent it will be repositioned in society.

Chapter Eight

Chile: Quality Assurance in a Context of Change

María José Lemaitre
National Commission for Programme Accreditation

A group of Chilean academics travelled to several countries in Asia, in order to learn about policy development in secondary and tertiary education. Every time Chile was mentioned, there was instant recognition, but it was normally limited to, 'Oh, Chile, long and narrow!'

This chapter is an attempt to go beyond the geographical oddity of the country and provide information on Chilean higher education. In it we will try to share the questions and challenges that have been faced during the last decade and, through an analysis of the decisions made, to explore the role of quality assurance in the development of the HE system.

A Brief Outline of Chilean Higher Education Provision

Structure and Size

Until 1980, Chilean Higher Education was organised into a relatively simple and consolidated system. There were two main public universities, each of which had opened branches in most provinces in the country, plus six private ones, three of them Catholic and three organised by philanthropic groups. Each of these institutions were created by law and were equally funded by the Government, which provided about 65 per cent of their total budget. Students paid a token fee and institutions obtained further resources through projects and services to the public and private sector.

In 1981 the system was totally transformed. The branches of public universities were turned into autonomous, regional public institutions, thus curtailing the social and political influence of the older public universities, and new legislation made it possible to establish private, HE institutions provided they could show that one of the previously existing universities (either the original eight or any of the new public regional ones) agreed to examine students and thus supervise the quality of teaching. Public funding was greatly reduced, students had to start paying fees and universities had to look for new sources of income. The system was further diversified into three institutional tiers: universities, which granted professional and academic degrees; professional institutes, which could offer professional but not academic degrees; and technical training centres, offering two-year technical degrees.

The three main features of the 1981 reform can be thus summarised as follows:

- atomisation of the system, through the splitting up of the large, strong public universities into 19 smaller institutions, and making possible the creation of new, private institutions. This was an obvious political move, whose objective was to reduce the influence of the public universities (which were a stronghold of opposition to the military government at the time) and to create regional centres that would further atomise and distribute power throughout the country. On the positive side, regional institutions were expected to develop strong links with local business and industry, and some of them have done so successfully;
- privatisation, not only through the possibility of establishing private institutions but mainly as a consequence of the reduction of public funding, thus making institutions highly dependent on private funds – and therefore, on market considerations – for their regular operation;
- differentiation, by creating a three tier system, with different kinds of institutions. This objective, which could have provided an interesting answer to the differentiation of Chilean society, was thwarted because the government immediately de-legitimised non-university institutions. In fact, the government turned all public professional institutes into universities and after identifying the more prestigious professional degrees, restricted their offering to universities only. Finally, by identifying all professional institutes and technical training centres with profit-making, private institutions, it sent a powerful signal against their educational legitimacy in a system that up to that time had included only public-funded institutions.

Since 1980 the system has experienced a rapid expansion, as can be seen from Table 8.1. The figures show a slow, concentrating trend, with universities the only sector to significantly increase its enrolment. Professional institutes show an apparent growth, but this, in fact, is the result of two institutions, which attract over 45 per cent of the students at that institutional level.

Table 8.1 Growth of institutions and enrolment in higher education institutions, 1980–2000

	1980		1990		1995		2000	
	No. inst.	Students	No. inst.	Students	No. inst.	Students	No. inst.	Students
Total	8	118,978	302	245,053	262	344,776	244	416,743
Universities								
– public*	8	118,978	20	131,702	25	231,161	25	212,125
– private	–	–	40	19,509	42	69,311	39	107,208
Professional institutes	–	–	81	40,006	69	40,980	60	107,208
Technical training centres	–	–	161	73,345	126	72,635	120	53,352

* Includes private universities with public funding.

Source: Ministerio de Educación, Chile, 2000.

Coverage of higher education has increased beyond the average for Latin American countries, even though admission to higher education continues to be quite selective. Students must also pay for their studies, and although the government provides scholarships and loans to the students enrolled in public universities, there is an economic bias affecting the student population.

Another feature that is important to mention is the change the student population has experienced in the last two decades. Chilean higher education has a long tradition of selectivity. Students entering public universities must pass a national entrance test, and are selected on the basis of their scores. Students whose scores are below the mean are not permitted to apply, and the scores of most of those enrolled are about one standard deviation above the mean. The development of private institutions meant that students who had lower scores had the opportunity to enter higher education, provided they had the means to pay the tuition fees.

New institutions also explored non-traditional delivery schemes, opening evening courses or establishing articulation mechanisms that made it possible for adults to enrol and either enter higher education for the first time, complete their studies or upgrade their degrees. As a consequence of these changes, the student population has evolved from the relatively homogenous higher income, higher scores, teenage students to a much more heterogeneous population with different cultural and economic backgrounds, older and in many cases made up of first-generation higher education students.

Funding Mechanisms

Until 1980, universities enjoyed what has been called the 'privileged autonomy' of institutions having most of their income assured from public sources, without being subject to any regulatory procedures. After 1980, higher education was obliged to develop new sources of funding, and to consider market opportunities as an important regulatory mechanism.

At present, funding for higher education institutions comes from different sources:

a) Public funding

- Direct public funding (AFD), which goes only to public institutions.
- Indirect public funding (AFI), that is distributed among all higher education institutions on the basis of the scores of the students they enrol.[1]
- Student aids, mainly scholarships and the support of a revolving loan fund.[2] The loan fund is restricted to public universities, while scholarships may be used in selected private institutions.
- Competitive funds, which are allocated for specific purposes (institutional development, research projects, quality improvement in selected areas). Some of these resources are allocated on a yearly basis, others can be spread over longer periods, normally limited to three years.

Public funding represents between 30 and 50 per cent of the total income of public universities, and seldom goes over 5 per cent in the private institutions.

b) Private funding

- Student fees.[3] This is the main source of private funding for most institutions, and it is the only source for most of the private ones.
- Services and contracts. Many institutions, especially the larger and stronger ones, are able to obtain resources through the sale of different services: research and studies, technical assistance, special courses, laboratory analyses, etc.

For most of the public universities, student fees provide between 35 to 50 per cent of their income. The balance is covered by income from services, which contributes about 35 per cent to the budget of the larger, research universities, and is lower in smaller institutions. In the case of private institutions, most of the resources come from student fees, and only the older, more consolidated institutions get funded either from the government (through competitive funds or AFI) or from services rendered.

c)   Mixed funding

Universities may also obtain resources from a third source: donations from private sources, who then recover as tax refunds 50 per cent of the money donated. Even though this is a minor source, it has helped many institutions renew and equip laboratories and other facilities.

Development of Quality Assurance Mechanisms

Quality assurance mechanisms have been slowly seen as necessary and have developed in different ways.

1) Initial deregulation In 1980, the opening of new higher education institutions was almost totally de-regulated. All a new institution needed to be certified was to show that an existing public institution had approved its study plans and was willing to examine students at the end of each term. In practice, this meant that public institutions imposed their own study plans on new, private institutions which operated in very different conditions, and applied their exams to the students in these institutions. The rule was that 50 per cent of the examined students had to pass, which was promptly arranged by presenting to the examination only those students who had already passed a previous, internal exam.

As a consequence of this lack of regulation, private higher education came to be seen as fit only for 'rich fools', that is, people who could afford to pay the higher tuition rates in private institutions, but could not pass the entrance tests to the public funded institutions.

2) Establishment of licensing procedures After 10 years of operation, the system was in trouble. Private institutions had failed to gain the necessary legitimacy to function as appropriate educational alternatives, and public institutions were clearly unable to cope with new demands for higher education. Therefore, in

1990 a new regulatory scheme was installed, which made accreditation mandatory for private institutions established after 1980. The Consejo Superior de Educacion developed such a system for universities and professional institutes. This scheme included self and external evaluation and has resulted in the closing of about 15 institutions, as well as the certification of autonomy of another 15. Technical training centres were supervised by the Ministry of Education and undergo a much less rigorous procedure. This, together with their chronic lack of funds, poor educational management and low social standing, may be a likely explanation for their slow development.

Public universities[4] are autonomous by law, and therefore are not subject to any regulation procedures. After 10 years of accreditation by the Consejo Superior de Educacion, private institutions may also gain a certification of autonomy. After this, neither the public nor the autonomous private institutions are subject to any regulation procedures.

For most of the 1990s, the relatively small number of private autonomous institutions and the high prestige of the public ones provided a measure of certainty regarding their quality. This is eroding as the number of private autonomous institutions increases and as there is increasing questioning of some of the public universities.

3) Voluntary programme accreditation A new scheme of programme accreditation is currently being established, which is voluntary and addresses only programmes offered by autonomous institutions.

This will be described further in the following pages.

Quality Assurance Mechanisms at the National Level

As has been briefly mentioned above, the present components of the Chilean QA system are the following:

Licensing for New Private Institutions

In March 1990, regulation procedures for new private institutions were established by law. This action was the result of the experience with deregulation in the 1980 resulting in 45 universities and 240 non-university higher education institutions being opened in that decade. The law created a new public, autonomous agency – the Consejo Superior de Educacion (Higher Council for Education) – and charged it with the establishment of licensing procedures for new private universities and professional institutes. At the same time, the licensing of technical training centres was assigned to the Ministry of Education.[5]

The agency The Consejo Superior de Educación has nine members, appointed by higher education institutions and other social organisations.[6] It is chaired by the Minister of Education and has joint funding, part of which comes from the national budget and part from fees paid by the institutions that apply for licensing. It has a technical staff and operates mainly through the work of consultants and evaluators hired for specific purposes.

The procedure The Consejo reviews all proposals for new, private institutions. It evaluates each proposal and either approves it or points out the remarks it may have. In the latter case, the proposal goes back to the institution, which has two months to adjust its proposal to the remarks of the Consejo and then re-submits it. The Consejo, then, makes a final decision on approval or rejection. If it rejects the proposal, the institution cannot be opened. If it is accepted, then it is legally recognised and may start operating, under the supervision of the Consejo.

During the first six year of operation of one such institution, it must submit an annual set of institutional data that includes academic and financial information. Students may be tested by external examiners sent by the Consejo and, at least twice, it is visited by a team of external assessors who analyse the development of the project and the degree to which it is fulfilling its goals. During this time, new programmes and degrees must also have the approval of the Consejo. Every year, the Consejo sends the institution an 'action letter' pointing out the perceived strengths and weaknesses, and the actions the institution must take. At the end of the sixth year, assessment is global, and if the institution is considered to have developed adequately, the Consejo certifies its autonomy. If not, supervision may be extended for a period up to five years, after which the institution is either certified as autonomous or closed down.

The Consejo may also, during the period of supervision, close down an institution if it considers that the institution is not acting on its recommendations.

Results of the licensing procedures applied by the Consejo can be seen in Table 8.2. In general, licensing procedures have gained recognition and acceptance. Institutions have had to accept supervision, learn to carry out self-evaluation and submit to external assessment. The closure of some

Table 8.2 Results of actions taken by the Consejo Superior de Educación, 1990–2000

	Created before the establishment of the CSE	Authorised between 1990 and 2000	Operating in 2001
Licensed new institutions			
– universities	43	5	37
– professional institutes	80	7	54
No. of institutions that have been closed[1]			
– universities			7
– professional institutes			10
No. of institutions certified as autonomous[2]			
– universities			11 (2)
– professional institutes			5 (6)

Notes

1 Institutions may close on their own. These figures refer only to those closed by decision of the CSE.
2 Institutions may be certified as autonomous under the original examination system. Between brackets is the number of institutions that obtained their autonomy without undergoing the process administered by the CSE.

institutions has not been without problems: students have had to be relocated, and the degrees obtained before closure, have suffered devaluation. But this has strengthened the system and those institutions that have their autonomy certified get a social validation that is extremely important in the competitive market higher education has become.

Programme Accreditation

The work of the Consejo Superior de Educación was important and had a strong impact on the growing social recognition and acceptance of quality assurance procedures within the Chilean higher education system. But its success also made it clear that the system was applying a double standard: new, private institutions were subject to supervision and had to comply with strong evaluation criteria in order to achieve autonomy. On the other hand, some institutions were born autonomous and, therefore, had never been subject to any kind of supervision. The behaviour of some of these institutions, and of some of the private universities once they achieved autonomy, showed that some quality assurance scheme would have to be established in order to maintain and guarantee standards.

Therefore, in 1998 the Ministry of Education decided to establish programme accreditation and to carry out a pilot project to help define the features of a national quality assurance system.

The agency The Ministry of Education established a National Commission for Accreditation, charged with designing an accreditation process and carrying it out; the experience gained could then be used in designing a national scheme for the accreditation of higher education offerings. The Commission has 14 members, appointed by the Minister of Education, and a technical staff in charge of coordinating and carrying out the accrediting procedures. Its funds come from the national budget, as part of a comprehensive programme for the improvement of quality and equity in higher education.

The procedure The Commission has organised its work in three areas:

- development of accreditation procedures. The Commission started work on those areas where there was a disciplinary or professional interest on accreditation among practitioners. It set up working groups, with the participation of faculty, professional associations and employers or users of the services of graduates in each specific field. The working groups[7] identify expected learning outcomes for each degree, and establish evaluation criteria to be applied to the units responsible for the degrees. They also identify prospective national and international evaluators, to act as peers in the external evaluation visits.

  Accreditation is voluntary. Programmes that ask to be accredited go through a self-evaluation process and then host a team of peer visitors, who validate the self-evaluation report. The Commission then makes a decision on accreditation, based on both the self-evaluation and the peer visitors' reports, which may take one of three forms: to accredit, to hold the decision until some actions have been taken or not to accredit. The decision is published only in the case of accredited programmes, at least during the pilot phase of the accreditation project.[8]

  Institutions may then ask for funds to comply with actions resulting from the accreditation process (regardless of the outcome), by applying to one of the competitive funds mentioned in the chapter on funding;

- development of self-regulation abilities in higher education institutions. It is obvious to the Commission that quality can only be the result of work carried out from the inside of each particular higher education institution, and that the most an external agency can do is to provide support, make urgent what institutions know to be important and offer assistance with materials and procedures. Therefore, an important part of the resources of the Commission is dedicated to promoting institutional actions oriented towards the establishment of self-evaluation capabilities, the development of information systems within institutions and improving management and planning abilities;[9]
- designing a proposal for a national accreditation scheme. The work done on the development and application of accreditation procedures has provided an experience that underlies the initial steps in the design of a national accreditation scheme. There is, in fact, a much greater interest in accreditation than initially anticipated and, despite contrary expectations, the establishment of learning outcomes for specific degree courses and the definition of generic evaluation criteria has been quite easy. On the other hand, self-evaluation has turned out to be a much slower process than initially expected, mainly because of the need to produce the supporting evidence and also because of intrinsic features of the self-evaluation process as designed. The Commission has identified a large number of areas in which decisions will have to be taken; yet, it is necessary to set up priorities in response to demands from the government and the higher education system, and on the basis of the gathered experience. This will be analysed further in the last section of this paper.

A Public Information System

Information seems to be essential in relation to quality assurance. Not only is it indispensable for institutions carrying out self-evaluation processes, it is also necessary for the public who have to make important decisions regarding higher education, and frequently must do so with little or no reliable background or data. The programmes that have already worked on self-evaluation have found that one of the most vexing problems they face is the lack of institutional data: these may be gathered at different levels of aggregation, are usually not comparable, are hard to find and they are even harder to follow for any number of years. If there is no accurate information base at the institutional level – whether data are gathered at the programme, department or other level – it is impossible to provide information to potential users of higher education.

This is even more of a problem in view of the changes that Chilean higher education has experienced in the last decades: for many people, the present structure is hard to understand and it is almost impossible to make sense of the huge number of programmes and institutions competing for students and faculty.

Within the higher education improvement programme of which the Commission is part, the development of an information system plays an important role; the Commission is in charge of the identification of the demands of different users of higher education, and of the development of ways and means to answer those demands.[10]

Quality Assurance at the Regional Level: the Experience of MERCOSUR

MERCOSUR, or common market of the South, is an economic agreement signed by four Latin American countries (Argentina, Brazil, Paraguay and Uruguay). An essential component has been the establishment of an educational sector to which Bolivia and Chile were invited as associated members. The Educational Sector of MERCOSUR (SEM) has as its main goals the development of a civic culture supportive of the integration process; training of the human resources needed to support regional and national development; and the harmonisation of educational systems.

SEM concentrates mainly at the school level, both primary and secondary, but it also considers the establishment of an Information and Communications System, dedicated to the provision of information, the development of common statistical indicators and a common glossary and a number of initiatives at the higher education level. One of these is the establishment of a regional accreditation scheme, which is in its initial stage.

The Ministers of Education of the six participating countries signed, within the framework of the SEM, a Memorandum of Agreement on the implementation of an experimental mechanism for the accreditation of degree programmes and recognition of degrees. The Memorandum selected three programmes for the pilot phase: engineering, medicine and agricultural studies.

The Memorandum stated that the accreditation scheme to be established had to abide by each country's legislation and respect the autonomy of HE institutions; it also must establish common quality parameters and criteria previously agreed upon by all countries and it could only be applied to institutions that were nationally recognised and either accredited by their own country or in the process of being so. Institutions submit voluntarily to

MERCOSUR accreditation, which is to be cyclical and must be carried out by a National Accrediting Agency, so appointed by the respective government. Agencies must base their decisions on the common criteria for each programme, previously approved by the Meeting of Ministers of Education, a self-evaluation report prepared by the institution and the recommendation of a peer review team. They can also set up their own procedures, which cannot contradict any of the above. The peer review team must include at least three members: one from the host country, and two from other member countries.

As a result of the process, all MERCOSUR countries – both members and associates – grant the accredited degree academic validity.[11]

The process has advanced quite rapidly, at least on the technical side. Guidelines for accreditation procedures have already been agreed on, as have a set of common criteria for the evaluation of the three selected degree programmes. These criteria have been validated in different institutions in the six countries, and should be brought to the attention of the next meeting of Ministers of Education in June 2001. There is also agreement on the criteria that must be followed for the selection of peer reviewers.

Nevertheless, there are a number of issues that remain unsolved. Some are unavoidable and unsolvable such as those that arise from the huge differences in size and complexity among member countries. Others will probably be solved in time but they depend mostly on political decisions. The most important is the fact that only three of the six countries have developed national quality assurance schemes; this could delay the start of the programme, even though the Memorandum specifically states that it will become operative if only two countries are willing to take part in it. This also affects the relationship between national and MERCOSUR accreditation, and the scope of the mutual recognition of accreditation.

In all, the effort to establish MERCOSUR accreditation has had a tremendous impact on the national higher education systems. It has pushed some of the more reluctant ones to adopt specific policies on the subject and has provided an international forum for a discussion on the main issues relating to quality assurance – something that in Latin America has been long overdue. The discussion of common evaluation criteria and quality standards for three specific degree programmes has also meant that the six countries have shared their outlooks on professional training, discovering, sometimes with surprise, that they are more different than originally thought. Finally, the international validation of these criteria and standards helped outline the essential standards that must be required of all programmes, which are desirable features of programmes and therefore should be on the agenda of all institutions seeking accreditation, and which are particular features of programmes in a given country. It has also pointed out the need to expand the discussion into other, related fields, such as the regulations governing professional licensure in the different countries and the need to find some common ground to ensure reciprocity.

Outstanding Issues

The development of a proposal on a national system for quality assurance brings to the surface a number of questions that must be dealt with. Answers to some have already been provided but most require further analysis, from both political and technical perspectives.

The first question refers to the *purpose* of the proposed quality assurance scheme: is it intended to weed out weak or poor institutions or programmes, to provide incentives to improve quality, to provide the public, government and clients a reliable report on the quality of the existing programmes and institutions? All of these purposes are important, but must be dealt with in very different ways.

The Consejo Superior de Educacion has effectively addressed the 'weeding out' process. Its approach to quality assurance is essentially one of supervision and control. On the other hand, the work carried out by the Commission in Chile has emphasised quality assurance at the programme level, while at the same time supporting quality improvement efforts at the institutional level. Should the proposed system proceed on these lines, it must consider actions to make institutions responsible (and accountable) for quality assurance at the institutional level, with the external agency providing support for the development of self regulation abilities and assuring the quality of specific programmes. Figure 8.1 represents this outlook, identifying for each instance the purpose, the frame of reference, the procedure for internal assessment and the instrument for external validation and accreditation.

In the second place, a decision must be taken whether *to focus on institutions, on programmes, or on a mixture of both*. Presently, the Commission has been working only at the programme level but there is a strong pressure on the side of many groups to develop institutional accreditation as a means to obtain public resources (especially for student loans and scholarships).

The third question refers to the *consequences of accreditation* and the incentives the government is willing to provide. Institutional accreditation could be a good mechanism to ensure that public resources – at least those

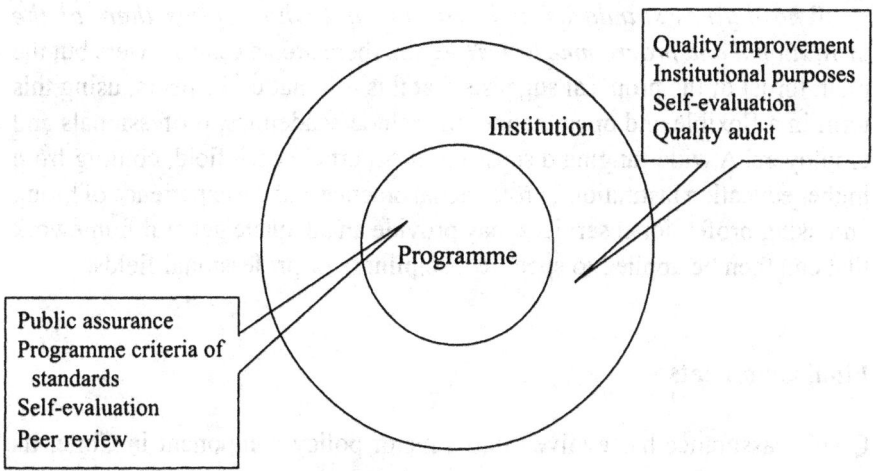

Figure 8.1 Elements of a quality assurance scheme

that benefit students – go to institutions that have adequate internal self regulation systems and, at the same time, would provide a strong incentive for the development of those systems. Other possible incentives to institutional accreditation are access to competitive funds, or bonus scores for projects that act on the outcomes of quality assurance procedures. At the programme level, accreditation provides applicants and employers with valid and reliable information about the quality of professional training, and at the international level, it is an important mechanism in the framework of free trade agreements, as a way of dealing with cross border services. Accreditation also has important market consequences, as it provides a 'seal of approval' that can be successfully marketed while trying to attract students.

Other questions refer to the operation of a quality assurance scheme: *who is responsible* for it? What is the role of government, and of the private sector? The preferred answer in this respect states that quality assurance at the national level is a public responsibility, especially if it is linked to public resources or international quality assurance. Nevertheless, this does not mean that it is a governmental task – it should also not be a university task, as it should be independent both from party and academic politics. The Commission is working towards a model whereby a public agency, with the participation of academics, professional associations and organisations of business and industry, is in charge of institutional accreditation. It could also accredit other accrediting agencies, who would then be responsible for quality assurance at the programme level.

Who defines standards and criteria, and who applies them at the institutional and programme levels? Again, there are no easy answers but the main thrust of the proposal suggests that this is a matter for peers, using this term in a flexible and open manner to include academics, professionals and employers. A wide-ranging discussion of experts in each field, coming from higher education institutions, professional practice and the experience of hiring and using professional services may provide an adequate general framework that can then be applied to specific disciplinary or professional fields.

Final Comments

Quality assurance has evolved into a major policy component in Chile. Its application and development have provided an opportunity to discuss which are permanent features of higher education institutions and which depend on specific features of institutional purposes. The work of the Consejo Superior provided needed regulation, after the experience of the 1980s showed that the market could not regulate for quality, and made evident the consolidation of many private institutions (at the same time it helped rid the system of institutions unable to develop effectively). Disciplinary and professional stakeholders are actively supporting the development of programme accreditation, and institutional accreditation that a few years ago seemed unthinkable, now is a probable occurrence.

The same can be said, with different degrees of development, of most countries in Latin America – Argentina, Brazil, Peru and Colombia alongside the work carried out in Paraguay, Uruguay and Bolivia under the aegis of the MERCOSUR. Each considers quality assurance an essential part of the higher education field.

This is especially important as higher education is, in the word of the Special Group on Higher Education and Society put together by the World Bank, 'indisputably the new frontier of educational development in a growing number of countries'. In this context, quality assurance can provide the means for growing numbers of people to increase their knowledge of a sector of society that is essential to personal, professional and social development, yet is usually little understood beyond a small circle of initiates.

Notes

1. Indirect public funding is linked to the scores obtained by 'the best and the brightest' students. After the scores for the admission test are calculated, the top 27,500 applicants carry with them a funding allocation to the institution where they enrol. The 27,500 highest scores are distributed into five equal groups of 5,500 students each. The students in the top group bring with them an amount roughly equivalent to one year tuition in a public university; the amount decreases to about one-twelfth of that amount in the bottom group. This is paid directly to the institution, and is not intended to benefit the students, but rather, to encourage quality in institutions. In practice, it has encouraged competition through marketing strategies, with little effect on quality; it has also provided strong incentives for institutions to open low cost, prestigious programmes (such as Business Administration, or Law), which typically attract students with top scores.
2. Students repay the loans after two years of graduation. Payments are dependent on income and the debt is extinguished after 12 years. The recovery rate has been historically low (about 47 per cent of the expected returns) but it is improving steadily.
3. Students pay, on average, between US$3,000–4,000 a year at the universities, about US$2,000 a year at professional institutes and US$1,000 a year at technical training centres.
4. Public universities, in this context, includes both public (state) universities and private universities created by law before 1980. These private universities are backed either by the Catholic Church or philanthropic organisations and are all fully non-profit institutions. All of these are funded on equal terms by the government.
5. This paper will not focus on QA procedures for technical training centres, which, anyway, are very similar to those described for universities and professional institutes.
6. Membership in the CSE is the result of appointments by state universities (1), private autonomous universities (1), private autonomous professional institutes (1), the council for science and technology (1), research organisations in the arts and sciences (2), the Supreme Court (1) and the Armed Forces (1).
7. There are currently working groups on Medicine, Architecture, Agricultural Studies, Veterinary Medicine, Biochemistry, Teacher Training, Psychology, Engineering and Law, as well as a generic group on Technical Degrees.
8. The Commission recognises the importance of publishing results of the accreditation process. Nevertheless, during this initial stage, it considers it is more important to attract institutions to the process, thus giving them the chance to carry out a self evaluation and to receive the input of a qualified visiting team. This provides the institution with significant inputs towards improvement, and makes it easier to achieve accreditation in the future.
9. Actions in this respect include study visits, funding specific projects within institutions, providing technical assistance from national and international consultants, helping selected officials to attend national and international seminars and workshops, etc.
10. A description of the work carried out regarding the development of a public information system can be found in J. Raczynski and M.-J. Lemaitre, 'Stakeholders in Higher Education: How to Deal with Complexity', presented at the VI INQAAHE Conference, Bangalore, India, 2001.
11. In order to practice a profession, each graduate must comply with any additional national regulations; the next step within SEM will address the recognition of professional qualifications.

References

Comision Nacional de Acreditacion de Pregrado (2000), *Manual para el Desarrollo de Procesos de Auto Evaluación*, Santiago, Chile.

Consejo Superior de Educacion (1998), *Ocho años de experiencia 1990 – 1998*, Santiago, Chile.

IBRD/The World Bank (2000), *Higher Education in Developing Countries: Peril and Promise*, Washington DC.

Ministerio de Educacion y Cultura (2000), *República Oriental del Uruguay, Educación y Mercosur*, Montevideo.

Ministerio de Educacion (1999), *República de Chile, Sistema de Educación Superior, Compendio Estadístico*, Santiago, Chile.

Sanyal, B.C. (1995), *Innovations in University Management*, UNESCO, Paris.

Chapter Nine

Strengthening Quality Assurance in Australian Higher Education

Kwong Lee Dow
University of Melbourne

In 2001, Australians celebrate 'a centenary of federation'. It was in 1901 that six colonies, now the states of New South Wales, Victoria, Queensland, South Australia, Western Australia and Tasmania, joined to create an Australian nation, the Commonwealth of Australia, with a new national constitution.

The ensuing division of legislative and financial responsibility between Commonwealth and state governments, more recently with the addition of two mainland territory governments, impacts most areas of Australian life including the organisation of education. To understand the drivers and the accountability for quality in Australian universities one needs to know that the legislative base for the universities in principally from the states in which they were founded, but the major source of revenue of public universities is from the Commonwealth government. So while the Commonwealth cannot legally require participation in schemes of quality assurance it may develop, it can require that participation as a condition for receiving funding. Much stems from this.

Clarification of the roles and operations of these different governments in Australia has led to collaboration between them through a Council of Ministers (the Ministerial Council on Employment, Education and Training and Youth Affairs) and when education policy in Australia is described as 'national' it usually means an agreement has been reached between all the governments through this Council. The Australian National Training Authority, for example, derives its authority from this collective body of all governments.

Australian educators refer to education 'sectors'. There is a schools sector, a higher education sector, and vocational education and training sector. Financial arrangements as between governments are complex and vary in each sector. Sometimes a fourth sector of adult and community education is identified. There is also early childhood provision across the age range 0 to eight years, with emphasis on preschool provision for three- to five-year-olds.

Recent Developments in Higher Education Quality Assurance

In 2000, education ministers representing state, territory and Commonwealth governments reached common agreement on two major enhancements for a quality assurance framework in higher education.

First was an agreement on a set of five regulatory protocols to ensure consistency in all jurisdictions to deal with:

- protecting use of the term 'university';
- regulating the operations of overseas higher education institutions in Australia;
- accrediting courses of providers who are not themselves self-accrediting institutions;
- ensuring responsibility by Australian institutions operating beyond the boundaries of their jurisdiction, that is, operating in other states of Australia and/or overseas;
- registering courses suitable for overseas students for whom, in consequence, visas to enter Australia would issue.

Second was to create a national audit body, the Australian Universities' Quality Agency (AUQA), as an independent company to audit self-accrediting universities on a 'whole-of-institution' basis every five years. The intention is to base each audit on self-assessment data generated by the institution itself, to check how effectively and professionally institutions monitor their own performance and use the information gained for planning and for improvement.

In announcing the AUQA, the Commonwealth Education Minister said:

> ... any new framework should take into account our federal structure, our universities and our history rather than slavishly adopting a British model (with its expense and intrusiveness), a US model (which involves industry regulation within a very diverse system) or a European model (with close links between universities and the state).[1]

While international readers will form their own judgements of Australian perceptions of their systems, this author sees that ministerial statement consistent with a statement made a decade earlier by a former minister from the other side of politics, when foreshadowing earlier audits of all Australian universities: '... some of the approaches adopted elsewhere ... run counter to the traditions of institutional autonomy in the extent of central intervention they involve ...'.[2]

The Nature of Higher Education Provision

Clearly and unambiguously, Australia now has a mass system of higher education. We appear a considerable distance from universal provision, though e-education initiatives and opportunities could lead to a reinterpretation of the meaning of universal provision. Some academically elite institutions remain from an earlier era, and in many respects, are strengthening. But by contrast with some countries and especially the United States, Australia has no wealthy universities.

While the mass system became visible with the disbanding of the binary system of universities and colleges of advanced education and the related amalgamations of the late 1980s, the move to a mass system really predates this. Today, Australian higher education can be summarised as mainly comprehensive public universities augmented by some specialist providers and a few small private universities. But the situation is not static.

As elsewhere, Australia is driven by the same powerful forces for globalisation, is positioning itself within the international fee-paying marketplace, and increasingly enrols mature aged students seeking a first university qualification, busy graduates in workplaces needing further qualifications efficiently delivered, and graduates seeking training in advanced research techniques often through industry partnerships increasingly with an eye to commercialisation.

Learning and teaching is in a stage of transformation with increasing development and adoption of multimedia and web-based courseware. Its value is at least as great for campus-based students as it is for distance education and off-campus students.

Funding issues dominate the agenda with ever more insistence. Surveys show the extent of increase in staff workloads (as in other walks of life). Issues now becoming routine include contracts relating to commercialisation, ownership of intellectual property, meeting compliance requirements, and managing arrangements by which staff can undertake outside work.

In 1989, 7.9 per cent of Australians had a university degree. In 1998, the figure was 14.3 per cent.

Quality Issues now Dominate

Funding issues and quality issues stand out as the dominant and enduring policy concerns of the decade.

This is partly explained by a community pressure to expand provision. It follows the increasing proportions who complete secondary school to find a limited youth labour market, with the decline not temporary, but sharp and probably permanent. There are cultural expectations. All talk is of a 'knowledge economy'. Political leaders proclaim education to be their top priority. There are aspirations of immigrant families and many first generation students in universities. And Australia has been conspicuously successful in attracting international students. Measured by our population, in the last decade we have outstripped other countries in this growth.

But growth only partly explains concerns about quality. When secondary schools were similarly expanding, new schools and additional classes had to meet the common criteria set and openly compared in state wide examinations which mark the completion of schooling in each Australian state and territory. Students, teachers and schools are judged on a common, though diverse, curriculum and at least partly common external assessments.

The outcomes of this assessment and certification are increasingly publicly accessible through school-based and student-based reporting in the media.

The culture of higher education stands in contrast. The universities inherit a tradition of autonomously determining who they teach, what they teach, how they teach, and how they judge exit standards. The former colleges, coming from a different tradition of course-by-course accreditation from an arms-length state agency, now through upgrading or amalgamation, have become self-accrediting universities.

This is an over-simple picture, as those active on academic boards of universities, and those active in professional organisations and industry based employer bodies which are involved in accreditation can readily attest. But it is roughly the picture in the public mind.

A further pressure for publicly accountable quality provision derives from students who today either make a real contribution to the cost of their higher education (some describe the HECS contribution as a part fee) or meet what is called a full-fee. Most overseas students in Australia pay full fees. Only a small minority remain supported through aid-based programmes. Domestic Australian students undertaking postgraduate coursework programs in many cases pay full fees, and in recent years, some Australian undergraduates, especially in professional courses for which entry is highly competitive, are able to obtain a fee-based place if their entry scores are just a little below those who gain a HECS-based place.[3]

The Higher Education Contribution Scheme (HECS) enables and indeed requires Australian students to make a contribution to costs, a fee to most people. This is not required to be met upfront on enrolment, does not require the taking of a loan, but is gradually paid back through the tax system when graduates reach certain thresholds in levels of earned income. Originally all students under this scheme contributed similarly, based on an average of the costs of different courses with a roughly one-fifth contribution to the averaged (across all courses) cost. The scheme has changed over time, requiring more of students, and considerably more from those taking costly courses (e.g. medicine) or courses which lead, on average, to high incomes (e.g. law).

In summary, three explanations exist for the recent increase in concern for accountability in quality standards. First, growth in students has led to an expanded system with inevitable queries about maintenance of earlier standards. Second, no external benchmark enables demonstration of comparability across institutions or across fields (and new fields) of study. Third, all Australian students feel they pay some fees, some Australians and nearly all international students pay full fees and so seek 'value for money'.

Quality Assurance at an Institutional Level

To reach good practice in quality assurance requires monitoring mechanisms that in turn depend on reliable and efficiently presented information. The task of developing, collecting and collating appropriate data sets and the subsequent publication of large quantities of complex statistical indices has become a core part of contemporary university management. This is not always visible to those articulate academics who complain of a cultural shift from the real business of teaching and research to form-filling and writing plans. Yet these days, formulating policies, setting priorities and measuring progress depends on trustworthy and strong bases of information.

Institutional leaders and many other decision-makers need well run planning offices, research offices, scholarship offices, and their counterparts across fields of finance, human resources, capital works and space management and so on. Without these groups functioning effectively, the baseline documentation for realistic strategic and operational plans and targets cannot exist.

One of the conditions for government funding for Australian universities is the annual submission of a Quality Assurance and Improvement Plan.[4] These are published and become public documents.

While the content and approach varies depending on the particularities of each university, there seems to have developed a broadly common format. Each Plan comprises about eight pages and each covers:

- how quality management fits within the planning structures of the institution and how quality links to institutional mission;
- quality assurance in learning and teaching;
- quality assurance in research and research education and training;
- quality assurance in community service activities;
- how quality judgements are made in management of resources: finances, human resources and capital programmes.

As an illustration, the following generalisations are made from the Plans for the 1999–2001 triennium, in the areas of learning and teaching and related student matters.

Surveys of student satisfaction with teaching are very widely used, perhaps are universal. They appear to be used regularly and across all parts of institutions. These surveys are particular to each university, cover individual subjects, each year or each semester. Some are particular to a faculty or school. In other cases, a common format across the university is used.

Also and separately reported are the institutional outcomes of a survey that is national in scope, administered a few months after graduation, and known as the Course Experience Questionnaire (CEQ).

A shift in emphasis is evident where institutions make increasing use of multimedia and web based curriculum courseware. The focus on effective teaching and the judgements of effectiveness of individual teachers, is replaced by the appropriateness of the course material, and whether it promoted effective learning. Behind this is the move from a small group of staff who design the course, select and present the content, and assess the outcomes, to a separation of course design, from courseware production, mentoring and direct student contact, and assessment.

By way of further illustration, taking the University of Melbourne as an example, the way that financial incentives and penalties operate to encourage improved teaching is described.

Four specific indicators of teaching quality are selected annually, a relative weighting of the four is agreed, and the package of items so weighted are scored separately for each faculty. The faculties with higher scores receive incentive funding in their annual budget, and those with the low scores are penalised by funds withdrawn. Overall, the exercise is budget neutral for the whole university.

The four indictors are:

- from a nine item survey used in every subject in every semester, the item,

'this subject was well taught' is assessed on a five point scale, and the totality of all assessments for all students in all subjects within a faculty is tabulated;
- two further items from the nine item survey are used. One relates to the extent that multimedia based technologies are helpful in teaching, and the other asks whether students are required 'regularly to make use of the internet';
- a measure of successful completion of first year through measuring the proportion of students who move direct to second year;
- a measure drawn from the CEQ (common national survey at the end of a course) which assesses the student view of the course overall.

These are different measures, and the outcomes tend to balance out in some faculties. In shifting A$1 million between faculties, where some gain, some lose and for some there is little impact, the greatest amounts gained and lost tend to be around A$200,000. This is a small component of most faculty budgets.

Internal Accreditation and Validation Processes

In internal institutional processes, the most common procedure is that for the approval of a new course, or the entry into a new field of study. While there are no common formal guidelines, the processes adopted by Australian universities are broadly similar. This is probably accountable from the movement of senior staff between institutions, the regular meetings of key groups under the auspices of committees of the Australian Vice-Chancellors' Committee (AVCC) and the influence of the procedures used by state accrediting bodies.

The key features are:

- document preparation by course proponents covering: justification and need for the course, likely prospective student groups and anticipated student numbers, including any 'marketing' already undertaken, what is increasingly called a 'business plan' or 'business case', detailed presentation of course structure, subject details, statements of who will do the teaching, the curriculum and assessment spelled out in quantity and methods often in considerable detail, teaching methods, facilities, equipment, library and information needs and so on;

- review of the documents by disinterested senior academics and others with experience in these processes, sometimes involving external people drawn from other universities, industry or the profession;
- reporting from the peer review through a committee structure to the senior academic body (often called the Academic Board) with that body's recommendation to the governing body (often called the Council) for final determination.

Once a course is in progress, there is usually a process for review after a stipulated number of years, as well as regular monitoring through particular performance indicators or benchmark measures as a part of boarder institutional monitoring.

It should be added that where professional accreditation is required by an external professional body (as, for example, in accountancy, engineering, law, medicine and health-related fields), the processes described may be more attenuated and complex but the basic principles still apply.

Quality Assurance Mechanism at a National and Regional Level

This section covers four areas of activity undertaken from a national rather than an institutional perspective. It includes initiatives undertaken by the Australian Vice-Chancellors' Committee (AVCC), the accreditation role of professional bodies, comparative guides for students developed in conjunction with the media, and the recent completion of a manual on Benchmarking for use in Australian universities. Specific initiatives led by and required by the Commonwealth Government will be dealt with in the following section.

AVCC

Over the past 15 years, AVCC as the peak organisation representing Australian universities nationally and internationally, has undertaken a range of initiatives to improve practice, increase consistency, and encourage more structured quality assurance mechanisms among member universities.

One early activity was to conduct and publish comparative reviews in specific disciplines of the standards of the final honours degree. The intention was to improve consistency of grading, discipline by discipline, across Australian universities.

Another initiative was to develop Codes of Practice in a number of areas, including university teaching, to offer individual universities a model against which each could assess and adjust their own practices and, if they wished, develop parallel codes. A recent addition has been a 'Code of Practice for Monitoring and Maintaining Academic Quality and Standards in Higher Degrees'. This is a detailed document with sections covering the responsibilities of institutions, responsibilities of departments, responsibilities of research supervisors and the responsibilities of research students. It has helpful sections on the conduct of thesis examinations, appeals processes, and intellectual property issues.

The AVCC is active in discussion between the Government and universities about the use of quality indicators and performance measures such as the Course Experience Questionnaire (CEQ), and the Graduate Destinations Survey (GDS), which tracks employment outcomes for recent graduates.

Professional Organisations

National professional organisations exist in many fields, and increasingly are undertaking accreditation exercises within universities. Professional bodies in the fields of medicine and its specialities, law, accountancy, engineering and architecture are long established with well-documented procedures. Similar activities now occur also in psychology and in social work.

In some cases the professional bodies have the power either to register or not register practitioners holding qualifications from particular institutions. For example, only graduates of medical schools registered by the Australian Medical Council (and graduates of other schools who have passed the AMC examinations) may be registered to practice in Australia and New Zealand.

In the case of AMC accreditation, the process extends over a considerable time. It begins with an institution receiving an extended questionnaire which covers curriculum content, teaching methods, assessment techniques, electives available, information on staffing, staff development, available resources including laboratories, hospitals and libraries.

Following consultation with the school concerned, an assessment team is appointed, normally at least six people, and normally some 12 to 18 months in advance of the institutional visit. During this lead up, a substantial submission is prepared and provided to the team members six months in advance. The main visit which is a week in length, is preceded by a preliminary visit from the team chair and executive officer.

After the visit a draft report is prepared, circulated to team members and when agreed, circulated to the school for its response. The team considers the response and forwards a final report to the AMC Accreditation Committee. The final report with comments from this Committee goes to the University for comment and when all due process is completed the AMC, and the Medical Council of New Zealand, decide whether to accredit, to accredit with conditions imposed, or to refuse accreditation. The final report becomes a public document.

Media Rankings and the *Good Universities Guide*

Readers are likely to be familiar with the league-table ranking of universities from media such as *The Times* (UK), US *News and World* and *Asiaweek*. These tables are constructed using quantitative performance indicators covering a range of activities, though they appear tailored toward the structures and context of the system operating in their own country.

The *Asiaweek* annual survey, for example, ranks over 70 universities from the Asian region. Australian universities feature, with eight universities in the first thirty ranked for 2000. The overall ranking is an aggregation of data drawn from five areas: academic reputation (peer rating by CEOs of the universities, some Asian corporations and a small number of non-participating foreign universities), student selectivity, faculty resources (very hard to get fair comparisons), research, and financial resources.

Given that such rankings are now a reality, institutions concerned with the problems of fair comparison, as to whether it is possible to compare like with like in quite different contexts, must make a judgement. Here is one recently expressed by an Acting Vice-Chancellor from a New Zealand university.

> For us, the decision whether to take part or not is something of a 'Catch 22'. If we don't then we could be accused either of not wanting to be accountable or of being afraid of the outcome. On the other hand, if we do participate, then we seem to be giving the survey a validity which it almost certainly doesn't warrant. [In the event, that University did participate, but it has modified or omitted some questions.][5]

While the Australian media do not independently rank Australian universities, they publish data provided by the Commonwealth government

(DETYA) of 'characteristics and performance' measures comparing universities on a range of different indicators. One annual publication which uses some of this information is *The Good Universities Guide*, a book of some 500 pages, intended for students, written in a user friendly style, and published in association with a leading Australian newspaper.

The *Guide* contains a series of rankings and rates of courses and campuses, mainly on a five point scale (the star system used to classify hotels, restaurants and films) as well as providing detailed accurate information about specific fields of study, comparing institutions, their campuses and their faculties and schools. Some of the separate criteria against which institutions are listed, are:

- prestige;
- extent of non-government earnings;
- student demand (how tough to get in);
- standing in research;
- proportion of non-school leaver entrants;
- staff qualifications;
- student-staff ratios;
- cultural diversity;
- getting a job;
- graduate starting salary;
- positive graduate outcomes.

Benchmarking Manual

The outcome of a project begun in 1998 led by former Vice-Chancellor, Professor Ken McKinnon, was the publication in 2000 of a comprehensive manual titled *Benchmarking in Universities*. The goal was to develop 'a robust, well-tested benchmarking manual in a common, easy-to-use format' for Australian and other universities. Many senior academics and most Australian universities were involved in some way with its development. There was consultation with the Commonwealth Higher Education Management Service (CHEMS) to draw on parallel experience with the hope that, as far as possible, common criteria could be established.

The manual provides senior executives in universities practical tools to ascertain performance trends in their institutions, which by agreement could be used with other universities who sought to make comparisons. The longer-term purpose is, of course, to implement improvements.

Sixty-eight benchmarks have been created 'to identify the most important aspects of contemporary university life in changing times'. The benchmarks cover:

- governance, planning, management;
- finance, physical infrastructure;
- external impact;
- learning and teaching;
- student support;
- research;
- staff;
- library and information services;
- internationalisation.

Recognising that 68 is a large number to monitor regularly, the most important 25 have been identified as a core set:

> to focus the minds of readers on the twin issues of what things matter in universities and how best to measure them ... Choices were based on the project leader's experience at Vice-Chancellor level and the views of project staff on the minimum canny Vice-Chancellors need to know to lead and get the most out of the universities they are heading.[6]

McKinnon makes the point that many indicators presented in the literature as 'performance indicators' are in fact not indicators of performance but are input indicators. Rather than use the input, process and output classification, McKinnon describes his 68 Benchmarks using a different typology as *lagging* (an outcome, such as reputation, which itself can lag where a university lives on past glories unsupported by current performance), *leading* (performance drivers) and *learning* (measures the rate of change).

The typology comes from the consulting firm of Arthur D. Little. 'It monitors the performance drivers and the rate of change aspects of the university functioning as well as the more familiar indicators.'[7]

To give an example, here is the Benchmark called Strategic Human Resource Planning. It is within a cluster of 'staff' benchmarks, and typed as 'Learning'.

Benchmark Rationale
Universities benefit from strategies that link human resource goals to overall strategic planning. Plans for the desired organisational culture, and policies for recruitment, retention, performance management, career development,

promotion, reward, tenure, occupational health and safety, and enterprise bargaining, are all linked.

Sources of Data
University Planning and Human Resource documents.

Good Practice
Entails a conscious linking and integration of the Human Resource policies and practices to achieve integration and consistency between recruitment, retention, career development, performance management, promotion, leave, grievance, salary and rewards, occupation health and safety to achieve the desired organisation culture. Enterprise bargaining should be consistent with these policies and practices and the university's key goals.

Levels (5 point scale)

Three levels are formulated
1. Human Resource policies unchanged for long periods. Policies separately developed without apparent relation to each other. Enterprise bargaining not undertaken as a coordinated activity. Enterprise bargaining time increased. Increasing staff turnover, insurance and other Human Resource costs.
3. Good individual policies, some integrated, others not. Links with Enterprise Bargaining not clear. Some reduction in time spent in enterprise bargaining. Static trends for costs of staff turnover, insurance and other HR costs.
5. Comprehensive policies and procedures, linking all aspects of HR with enterprise bargaining and with the university's key goals. Reduced time spent in enterprise bargaining. Reducing trend in expenses associated with staff turnover, insurance and other HR costs.

Role of the Commonwealth Government

Without doubt, the most powerful external influence on the behaviour and mode of operation of Australian universities that receive government funding is the government itself, acting through its Department of Education, Training and Youth Affairs (DETYA). This has been so for around three decades.

A recent statement from the AVCC explains the funding impact this way:

> In 1997 Australia's direct public investment in higher education as a percentage of GDP was on the average for OECD countries. Our private investment, mostly student HECS and fees, was above the average, exceeded only by the United

States, Korea and Japan. Over the period 1990 to 1996 total investment has grown in Australia as in nearly all OECD countries, but Australia experienced a much stronger growth in private investment than many. In other words, the government was largely continuing to substitute public investment with fees during this period. After 1997, the full impact of the most recent substitution took effect. This is likely to mean that later OECD tables will show that Australia is even worse than average in terms of the percentage of GDP spent by government on universities.[8]

In the University of Melbourne, for example, 17 per cent of total income comes from student fees (fee paying overseas students, fee paying postgraduate coursework for Australian students, and small but growing number of Australian undergraduates who enrol for fee based rather than HECS based places) and a further 13 per cent is attributable to HECS payments.[9]

Earlier University Quality Audits

Though generally not compulsory, all the Commonwealth funded universities in Australia participated in a distinct program for quality assurance in 1993, 1994 and 1995. The trigger was a report, *Achieving Quality*, from the (then) Higher Education Council to the (then) Minister for Higher Education which found:

> Quality audit mechanisms are conspicuous by their absence in Australia ... while current processes and mechanisms for system level assessment in Australia fulfil certain specific and useful purposes in relation to quality assurance, they are not sufficiently systematic, comprehensive in their coverage, nor representative enough of all stakeholders, to provide quality assurance for the system as a whole.[10]

In response, a *Committee for Quality Assurance in Higher Education* was formed to instigate a programme of audits that:

- were based on institutional self-assessment;
- were focused on assessment across the whole university, rather than on particular disciplinary fields;
- led to additional funding being provided by the government dependent on the extent to which institutions displayed a high level of quality in relation to their mission and goals;

Strengthening Quality Assurance in Australian Higher Education 137

- resulted in each university being audited in each of the three years.

The significant financial rewards available, and the concern to enhance and protect institutional reputations influenced the pace of change over these years. Peter Williams, then head of the audit group in the UK Higher Education Quality Council said at the time he believes the process introduced greater cultural change in Australia than in England and elsewhere.[11]

The Committee itself later observed that its work should be seen 'as a further step in a sequence of university and government actions over many years, rather than an isolated instance of government intervention'.[12]

Now, in hindsight, the Committee can be seen as the forerunner to the new AUQA.

Certainly since this time much baseline data has accumulated and been published. Three major data sources have enabled DETYA to regularly update and extend its 'Characteristics and Performance of higher education institutions'. These are:

- DETYA Higher Education Statistics collections, now separately published as 'Students', 'Staff' and 'Finance' collections;
- DETYA Research Data Collection;
- data on graduate employment from the annual Graduate Destination Survey and data from a student opinion survey, the Course Experience Questionnaire, taken by new graduates a few months after course completion.

Various working parties have, over the years, turned these data sets to a series of quantitative comparative indicators, published annually or biennially, and so forming a useful time series.

Grouping Australian Universities into Clusters

Attempts have been made to use selected elements of this data to show a clustering of Australian universities around common characteristics. By selecting different orientations of data, the clustering can be shown to vary a little.

Perhaps this was done to counter an emerging informal classification of research intensive universities (the now well delineated Group of Eight), universities which derived from large and well-established Institutes of Technology in the mainland capital cities (the Australian Technology Network), regional universities (characterised by their service to geographic regions and their student catchment areas) and a diverse group of other institutions.

A recent alternate characterisation has been drawn by two respected and independent commentators who delineate:

- sandstones, the oldest foundations in each state;
- redbricks, strong post second world war universities who 'have had less time to accumulate status benefits';
- gumtrees, founded between 1960 and 1975, 'many sites were planted with natives in contrast with the English gardens of the colonial period';
- unitechs, largest of the old CAEs in five states with strong vocational orientation, with architecture "characteristically ugly, ranging from a grimy early Fordism/Taylorism, to utilitarian modern';
- new universities, heterogeneous post-1986, 'In their buildings, utilitarian recency combines with secondary school leftovers from the CAE period'.[13]

Controversial Indicators

Much of the published data drawn from statistical collections which compare universities are seen by the institutions as descriptive characteristics rather than achievement (or performance) measures and so are not a source of controversy. But ongoing tensions continue where the government insists on the continuing use by all universities of a particular survey from which institutional comparisons are drawn.

The *Course Experience Questionnaire* (CEQ) is a 25 item instrument which has been used in each of the past nine years to survey all graduates from Australian universities a few months after the completion of their courses. It is applied across all fields of study and across all universities. The items are clustered around topics described as – good teaching, clear goals, appropriate workload, appropriate assessment, development of generic skills, and overall satisfaction.

The universities acknowledge that the data so collected provides useful comparative indicators of quality for prospective students as well as for the universities themselves and for the government. They are concerned, however, when the data from quite disparate fields of study is collapsed into a single indicator for an institution as a whole, and they are concerned where they believe inappropriate comparisons are being made between institutions with very different profiles.

A parallel questionnaire is now in development to survey those who have recently completed postgraduate research degrees, the *Postgraduate Research Experience Questionnaire* (PREQ). Items will rate experience of supervision, skill development, intellectual climate, infrastructure, thesis examination and overall satisfaction.

Here too, concern is being voiced. Unlike the undergraduate coursework programs which involve large numbers of subjects and teachers, because the research postgraduate experience is heavily influenced by a single supervisor, the outcome is likely to be highly dependent on particular individuals. And, while any idiosyncratic responses in the undergraduate CEQS is likely to be averaged out by the majority in a class, this is less possible when a department or research centre has a small number who would complete in any one year.

Some universities conduct separate additional surveys of graduate satisfaction. The University of Melbourne, for example, surveys its graduates two years and five years after graduation, collecting data on employment circumstances as well.

Another initiative being led by the government is the development of tests to measure the learning of generic skills that occurs during university education. For some time major employers have highlighted the priority they attach to broad general skill development, and in consequence a *Graduate Skills Assessment* (GSA) instrument is under development, which first will require identification of a set of valued generic skills which could be effectively assessed at entry and exit level. The skills are likely to include better communication, critical thinking, problem-solving, interpersonal understandings. A likely format is a two-hour multiple choice test and a one hour written test. The development is being viewed with some scepticism at this early stage.

Private Providers, Distance Education and Non-traditional Modes of Delivery

In Australia at present the scale of private provision is small. A survey in 1999 found 86 private providers of higher education courses registered in Australia. Of these, 79 responded and reported catering for around 30,000 students or, in equivalent full-time units, a little under 20,000. This is 3.4 per cent of the total equivalent full-time load. It is made up of professional and industry associations (33 per cent), theological colleges (17 per cent), niche operators (28 per cent) and private universities (22 per cent).[14]

Some of this private provision will be mainstream or traditional in modes of delivery and in educational philosophy. It may be that greater stimulation towards e-education and its transformation of learning and teaching is coming from institutions described as 'traditional'. But the challenge of the communication and information technologies now is pressing and fundamental.

This challenge has been sharply put by the Vice-Chancellor of the University of Melbourne, Professor Alan Gilbert, who also initiated and now chairs the group of international research intensive universities known as Universitas 21.

> Universities are probably under the most severe threat in their 900 year history because there is a threat to their monopoly. For the first time non universities are saying, 'we will offer awards and not bother with being accredited', and are competing with universities in the education market. They are able to do so because demand is greatly outstripping supply. Traditional universities are misguided if they are complacent.[15]

These new providers, whether corporate providers, virtual universities, for-profit providers or institutions like Universitas 21, are responding primarily to working adults seeking practical and immediate knowledge and skills, delivered efficiently to take account of other demands on their energy and their time. In so doing however, these new institutions and new approaches strike at the heart of mainstream universities for they call into question their cost structures, their modes of operation, their need for expert staff on long-term appointments, their capital provision and the investment that implies, and their accountability and quality assurance mechanisms.

Though we are at only the beginning of formulating quality assurance arrangements to fit these new circumstances, it is clear that the transformative effects on teaching and learning will impact no less on campus-based, full-time and young students, as it will on the off-campus students with quite different personal profiles.

In Conclusion

Undergraduate programmes have expanded in response to a broadening range of school leavers and adults seeking first-time higher education and the sector draws larger numbers of international students now from over 200 countries.[16] Postgraduate course work programmes have stabilised, with a substantial proportion of employed people meeting the full costs of these courses. Research education and training is expanding as is the partnership between academics, researchers and industries.

The quality assurance framework was comprehensively tested with every university having experienced three consecutive years of audits. Each university has a regular annual interaction with government on quality issues (the profiles process) in addition to monitoring through surveys and information flows.

The framework will be significantly strengthened by the establishment of an Australian Universities Quality Agency, and by the agreements between all governments which have led to a set of protocols to ensure consistency in all aspects of accreditation and across the country.

Notes

1 'Quality Assured: a new Australian quality assurance framework for university education', statement by the Hon. Dr D.A. Kemp, 10 December 1999 at a seminar on the new quality assurance framework, subsequently printed, p. 6.
2 Australian Government Publishing Service, *Higher Education: Quality and Diversity*, policy statement by the Minister for Higher Education and Employment Services (1991).
3 In consultation with each university, the government agrees the number of HECS-based places, by field, that it will fund. Universities choose whether or not to make additional fee-based places. If they do, the government caps the number, usually at not more than one quarter of HECS-based places, per course.
4 See, for example, *The Quality of Australian Higher Education 1999*, Department of Education, Training and Youth Affairs (DETYA).
5 See *Vic News*, the April 2000 newsletter of the Victoria University of Wellington, reported in *Siftings*, May 2000 newsletter of the New Zealand Universities Academic Audit Unit.
6 *Benchmarking in Universities*, DETYA 2000, section 12.1.
7 Ibid., section 1.4.
8 *Our Universities Our Future*, AVCC 2000, section 3, p. 6.
9 The University of Melbourne 2001, Budget, p. 5. Data will be subsequently published in an Annual Report, and in Strategic Plan Perspective 2001.
10 AGPS, *Higher Education: Achieving Quality*, Report of the Higher Education Council (1992), p.76.
11 Cited in 'Quality in Universities', the Sir Robert Menzies Oration on Higher Education, Professor Brian G. Wilson.
12 Ibid.
13 Marginson, S. and M. Considine (2000), *The Enterprise University: Power, Governance and Re-invention in Australia*, Cambridge University Press, p. 189.
14 See Louise Watson, *Survey of Private Providers in Australian Higher Education 1999*, DETYA 2000, Executive Summary.

15 Quoted in *Guardian Weekly*, 11–17 January 2001, by Donald MacLeod, 'Cashing in on Clever Business Plans', 24.
16 DETYA, Higher Education Report for the 2001–03 triennium. Section 1.0 says that 'overseas student enrolments ... are projected to total around 117,000 in 2003, up 200 percent on 1995. Australia now attracts higher education students from 207 countries'.

Bibliography

Official Government Publications

Department of Education, Training and Youth Affairs (DETYA) (2001), 'Higher Education Report for the 2001–03 Triennium' (earlier annual reports are also available).
DETYA (2001), 'The Characteristics and Performance of Higher Education Institutions 2000: Preliminary Report'. Earlier compilations of data are also available, e.g., DETYA (1998), 'The Characteristics and Performance of Higher Education Institutions' (Occasional Paper Series 98–A).

Commissioned Government Publications

Anderson, D. et al. (2000), *Quality Assurance and Accreditation in Australian Higher Education: an assessment of Australian and international practice*, DETYA.
Cunningham, S. et al. (2000), *The Business of Borderless Education*, DETYA.
Graduate Careers Council of Australia (1999), *Course Experience Questionnaire 1999* (there are related publications and earlier annual publications).
Harman, G. and V.L. Meek (2000), *Repositioning Quality Assurance in Australian Higher Education*, DETYA.
Higher Education Council (1996), *Performance-based Funding of Universities*, Commissioned Report No. 51, National Board of Employment, Education and Training.

Independent Commentaries

Ashenden, D. and S. Milligan (2001), *The Good Universities Guide to Universities, TAFE's and Private Providers*. Hobsons Australia, Western Australia, published in association with *The Age* newspaper. Earlier editions are available, published in association with *The Australian* newspaper.
Marginson, S. (1997a), *Educating Australia*, Cambridge University Press.
Marginson, S. (1997b), *Markets in Education*, Allen and Unwin.
Teather, D.C.B. (1999), *Higher Education in a Post-binary Era*, London: Jessica Kingsley Publishers.

Chapter Ten

External Quality Assurance in Higher Education in South Africa

Danie Jacobs
Certification Council for Technikon Education (SERTEC), South Africa

Introduction

As in so many areas of South African life, higher education has undergone profound changes in the post-apartheid era since 1994. Traditionally, higher education had been provided through a range of institutions: universities, technikons, teacher-training colleges, agricultural colleges, nursing colleges and technical colleges. Even within a particular type of institution, such as the universities, clear divisions could be identified between those that were predominantly for Afrikaans and those for whites where English was the medium of instruction. The latter were, on the whole, well-established and well-funded institutions while the former had generally only come into being after the 1959 legislation providing higher education for a small proportion of the black population. Within this setting there were few controls over higher education even though the former Department of National Education had responsibility for financial matters and, in principle, for standards. So many different types of institution with differential and discriminatory funding regimes and differing degrees of autonomy in different 'homelands' and with different racial mixes all came together to produce a system that was fragmented and lacking in quality assurance mechanisms.

The universities were required to seek state permission for new programmes and, indeed, for new organisational structures such as the formation of a new faculty but they enjoyed a considerable degree of autonomy. This was evident in admissions, mode of teaching, assessment and the awarding of qualifications; in fact, through the whole educational process. Monitoring of quality only took place where professional bodies were involved such as in medicine, dentistry or accounting. In these traditional professions, the professional bodies had the authority to set admissions criteria, to confirm the curriculum and to recognise the qualifications.

The technikons operated differently and had been designed to be quite different from the universities in that their focus was on scientific disciplines, many of which provided a professional training (in engineering, for example) and were very career-orientated.

The technikons, in their desire to deliver higher education and training of better quality and to become more competitive in the higher education sector, in the 1970s and 1980s requested greater autonomy from the authorities in respect of the conduct of examinations and certification of successful candidates. Examinations were gradually transferred from the Department of National Education to the technikons over a period of 10 years up to 1988.

As shown below, very significant and fast-moving changes are currently occurring in the South African quality assurance system. Before addressing these, it is instructive to discuss in some detail how the one system for one part of higher education has been operating – quality assurance in the technikons.

Certification Council for Technikon Education (SERTEC)

The establishment of a certification body to be responsible for the manipulation of examination results and the awarding of certificates to successful candidates was recommended after intensive local and overseas investigation by officials of the then Department of National Education. The Certification Council for Technikon Education Act, 1986 (Act No 88 of 1986), was passed whereby SERTEC was established as a certification body. The first Council was appointed in 1988 and the office of SERTEC was established with the appointment of the Executive Director on 1 April 1989.

The Council decided at its first meeting in July 1988 that monitoring of the quality of education in the technikons by means of visiting evaluation committees, as it is done in many countries of the world, should be adopted as the *modus operandi*, as statistical techniques were not available for the manipulation of examination results in fifteen different examinations and with small numbers of candidates in each. It was considered that such central manipulation of examination results would be detrimental to the improvement of quality and the autonomy of the technikons.

By 1993 SERTEC had became an accreditation body, while retaining the certification function. No technikons or agricultural colleges have certification authority in terms of current legislation, except for non-formal short courses.

Requirements for the monitoring of the quality at technikons were drafted in cooperation with the Committee of Technikon Principals. All requirements and procedures were documented in a "Manual for the Evaluation of Standards at the Technikons". The requirements and procedures have been regularly updated in terms of the experience of past evaluations. The monitoring of the quality of technikon education and training commenced in 1991, in terms of such rules and regulations determined by the Council. Self-evaluation as a basis for the monitoring of education quality was introduced at the technikons in 1996. The partial institutional and program levels of quality monitoring were introduced from the start.

Evaluation committees, one per programme, evaluate programmes at technikons in a four-year cycle. Each committee comprises a person from the same field of expertise from another technikon as convenor, representatives from the relevant professional organisations, employer representatives and a current or past student. The unduplicated headcount of persons involved in such committees since 1991, currently number approximately 9,000. If persons involved are counted for every exercise they were involved in, the number of participants approaches 18,000. Approximately 120 professional organisations participated and agreed that separate monitoring of standards by them, even if they have statutory authority to do so, was unnecessary. SERTEC regards the participation of the professional organisations as a necessary and important component of the evaluation activities of the Council.

Representatives of employers and professional organisations participated at no expense for SERTEC. Only the travelling and accommodation costs of the convenors from other technikons, of the Council member and the office official that accompanied the visits, were paid for.

Committees are supplied with the necessary information from the office of SERTEC and copies of the self-evaluation reports of the technikon a month before the visit. Up to 50 programmes are evaluated per semester in terms of a prearranged schedule. Committees draft reports with recommendations on-site. Such findings are reported in a public session on the second day of the two-day visit to the technikon management and staff. Technikons are provided with an opportunity to challenge any statements that are factually incorrect. At the next Council meeting the Council considers the recommendations of the committees and communicates any decisions to the rectorate by correspondence.

Depending on the seriousness of the shortcomings reported, Council might take one of the following decisions:

- the technikon may be accredited to offer such a programme for the next

period of four years;
- it may be requested to report in writing to Council within one year on the remedying of such shortcomings;
- it may be revisited within 18 months; or
- it may be requested to close a programme that could not deliver persons with adequate training for the purpose intended in the programme. Technikons appear, perhaps understandably, to prefer closing such programmes themselves without being instructed to do so.

Technikons respond very positively to the decisions of Council. One technikon decided to close a programme as a result of the outcome of an evaluation visit. In most cases technikons make an effort to improve the situation.

The above description comprises the program assessment component of the SERTEC model. It has been accepted by technikons, the industry and professional organisations. Experience has shown that the accountability and improvement features of such external evaluation are both met.

Evaluation committees for institutional level evaluation

At the beginning of each cycle, committees are appointed to evaluate by visits to the technikons, the following aspects at institutional level of technikon education and research:

- Examinations administration;
- Resources centre services;
- Experiential learning;
- Research capacity and maintenance;
- Internal quality assurance policies, procedures and implementation.

The last mentioned committee was activated in 1999. Some professional organisations and employers are invited to serve on such committees under the convenorship of persons from other technikons.

At the end of each cycle the activities at the satellite campuses and other institutions with which the technikons have agreements for the offering of technikon programmes are evaluated by means of on-site visits. The number of such "satellite campuses" has increased from 29 to more than 50 during the last four-year cycle. This component comprises the partial institutional level audits conducted by SERTEC. It is intended to expand this to technikon activities other than the education and research in the future.

Academic Committees for Infrastructure Evaluation

With the introduction of undergraduate and postgraduate technological degrees at the technikons in 1994, the Minister of Education commissioned the SERTEC Council to evaluate the infrastructure of the technikons on application to offer such programmes and to certify the adequacy thereof with a view to the successful offering of such degree programmes. A mechanism was developed for the conduct of such evaluations, which was based on a documented application. Visits to the technikons did not take place for this purpose, unless the evaluating committee felt it necessary.

Fifty Academic Committees have been appointed for the purpose of such infrastructure evaluation, each with two members and none from within any technikon. Those committees are still functioning as applications are received. Approximately 750 such applications have been evaluated since 1995. Technikons pay separately for this service.

The Agricultural Colleges

The twelve agricultural colleges have come under the auspices of SERTEC quality monitoring in terms of the Certification Council for Technikon Education Amendment Act, 1993 (Act No. 185 of 1993). The first visits by evaluation committees were conducted in the first semester of 1995 with the second cycle of visits starting in 1996. As an outcome of the slow response from the provincial Departments of Agriculture, it was decided to change the four-year cycle of visits to the agricultural colleges to a two-year cycle. Four or five agricultural colleges are visited annually over the cycle of two years. The emphasis has since been shifted toward internal quality assurance with external validation, leading to accreditation. The Council decided to withdraw its certification authority from one agricultural college as it was found after two visits that it is incapable of providing education of the minimum required quality.

The SERTEC Council has initiated developments in quality assurance in agricultural colleges and has gradually shifted the emphasis towards internal quality assurance. Self-evaluation reports of the same extent as required of the technikons, have been introduced in the agricultural colleges since 1997.

Attempts at Further Expansion

Attempts have been made in 1992 and in 1996 to have the Act amended to extend the functions of SERTEC to higher education institutions other than the technikons. In 1993 Parliament approved the Certification Council for Technikon Education Amendment Act, 1993 (Act No 185 of 1993). In terms of that Amendment Act only the 12 agricultural colleges were included under the auspices of SERTEC. The agricultural colleges are currently being evaluated for the second time.

Discussions have been held since 1992 with the technical colleges (higher education sector), colleges of nursing and private colleges to win their support for internal and external quality assurance mechanisms to be introduced in their systems. They all showed interest at the time in quality monitoring and accreditation by SERTEC. Officials of the Department of National Education at the time did not, however, consider such further expansion of activities necessary. That decision has since been shown to be questionable.

The attempt in 1996 did not succeed as the National Commission on Higher Education began functioning and the final viewpoint of government on the findings of the Commission, made such amendment superfluous. The Council of SERTEC has since pledged its full support for the establishment of the Higher Education Quality Committee (see below) and the development of its functions.

Since 1998 SERTEC has been requested to conduct external quality monitoring at Polytechnics in the SADC region. Agreements have been entered into with the Polytechnic of Namibia, the Lerotholi Polytechnic in Maseru, Lesotho and the Bulawayo Polytechnic in Zimbabwe. The first two have been evaluated and evaluation will commence at Bulawayo in March 2001.

The Effect of SERTEC Evaluation

SERTEC started functioning in 1988 with the first meeting of the Council and from 1989 it was introduced to the general public, employers, professional bodies and the technikons themselves. It was indicated to the technikons what the requirements would be in that SERTEC would cooperate with the Committee of Technikon Principals and all technikons by starting to prepare documentation to prove that they satisfied the norms and standards set by SERTEC.

There is a general feeling that the preparation of such documentation had a positive effect on the technikons. The fact that they had to be evaluated by external parties also had the effect that technikons have brought matters to order and have improved their internal situations to such an extent that the technikons of the SERTEC era are in better standing in the eyes of the professional bodies and the employers than those of the pre-SERTEC era.

The following positive effects of the existence of SERTEC may be listed:

- As indicated above the professional bodies have given their cooperation to a greater extent than was anticipated. All have indicated that they do not see the need to perform their evaluating functions in terms of current legislation separately, but that they will coordinate it with the SERTEC evaluation visits. Some professional bodies have for the first time taken cognisance of the circumstances pertaining to technikon education and have pledged financial and other assistance to improve the equipment in some of the laboratories. Some have also undertaken to assist with the placement of students in experiential training workstations. Where necessary, they have extended the generic questionnaires supplied by SERTEC to suit the purposes of registration of practitioners. No professional organisations have insisted on independently evaluating the programs they have an interest in, except for follow-up visits requested by SERTEC.
- Most of the employers' representatives have for the first time taken cognisance of the financial and other constraints under which technikons function. Some of them have also pledged assistance with the provision of equipment and the placement of students in experiential training work placements. Approximately 4,000 employer representatives (unduplicated headcount) have participated in the two completed cycles of visits to the fifteen technikons and eleven agricultural colleges. This has greatly contributed to the transparency of the exercise and the accountability of the institutions in respect of quality education.
- In the case of a small number of instructional programmes some technikons were requested to improve the standards of certain examination papers. One technikon was requested to introduce formalised laboratory sessions in its Civil Engineering programme in order that students could gain hands-on experience. Such formalised laboratory sessions are traditional in technikon engineering programmes. One technikon terminated the services of a senior staff member, partly as a result of the lack of leadership in the relevant School as pointed out by the SERTEC evaluation committees. One technikon was requested to introduce an examinations audit unit to ensure the correct handling of examination marks. One technikon rebuilt its entire photographic section as a result of SERTEC requirements.

- Two technikons could not pass an accreditation evaluation for a particular programme. Another technikon decided to spend money and energy on the improvement of the situation. In a follow-up visit the situation was found to be vastly improved and the Council approved accreditation thereof. The other technikon decided to close the programme.
- The necessity of improved staff qualifications, further stocking of libraries and an improvement in the staff participation in research projects and research supervision, with a view to further developments in technikon education, was brought to the attention of all technikons after the visits of the SERTEC evaluation committees. It is a SERTEC requirement that staff must be higher qualified than the levels at which they lecture.
- Greater openness developed between the staff members of different technikons and between the technikons, the professional bodies and the employers as a result of the evaluation visits of the SERTEC committees. The requirements of transparency of the process and the accountability of the education provision have been adequately met by this process.
- The Minister of Education in 1995 approved the introduction of technological degree programmes at the technikons on the levels of B Tech, M Tech and D Tech. It may be accepted that the quality monitoring by SERTEC has contributed to the improvement in the quality of education at the technikons and that this led to the approval of the degree structure by the Minister.
- Technikons have pledged general support for the continuation of external quality monitoring by SERTEC. The expertise and experiences gained by the Council will, however, probably be absorbed into the new Higher Education Quality Committee (see below), which will be responsible for quality assurance in all sectors of higher education in South Africa.

SERTEC has pleaded since its inception for the improvement of credit recognition and mobility of students between institutions. It therefore welcomed the establishment of the South African Qualifications Authority (SAQA). The South African Qualifications Authority Bill was, interestingly, drafted by the legislators on the basis of the contents and aims of the Certification Council for Technikon Education Act, 1986 (Act No 88 of 1986). SERTEC provided assistance in this regard.

The requirements and procedures for the preliminary accreditation of private higher education institutions with a view to conditional registration with the Registrar of Private Higher Education Institutions were formulated. Such requirements were based on the infrastructure evaluation SERTEC conducts at technikons.

In anticipation of the establishment of the Higher Education Quality Committee, SAQA accepted the role of a quality assurance body for the private higher education institutions. SAQA has contracted SERTEC and the Quality Promotion Unit of SAUVCA to conduct such preliminary accreditation.

Clearly from this review, much needs to be done in South Africa for its higher education quality assurance systems to be considered comparable with many other countries. It would appear that only the technikons have been subject to the same kind of evaluation considered normal elsewhere. However, the situation is changing rapidly and, indeed, in recent years there has been an astonishing degree of activity in an attempt to raise quality assurance mechanisms and systems to those prevailing in, say, Europe and the USA.

The Changing Pattern of Quality Assurance

The lack of coherence amongst the various branches of higher education in South Africa helped to promote the establishment by government in 1995 of the National Commission on Higher Education in an attempt to develop a national structure from the disparate sectors. Quality was high on its agenda not simply because of the perceived need for transparent internal reviews but also because of the need to establish a different kind of relationship between higher education institutions and government. The Commission subsequently produced its own Report as well as being partly responsible for drafting the Green Paper relating to the transformation of higher education emanating from the Department of Education in 1996. Again, quality and quality assurance were high on the agenda. The Education White Paper that followed in 1997, "outlines a comprehensive set of initiatives for the transformation of the higher education through the single coordinated system with planning, governing and funding arrangements" (Department of Education, 1997, p. 7). It was from this that the current arrangements came about. Before examining these, however, it is worth pointing to a development at about the same time.

This development proved to be less successful than envisaged and involved the establishment of the Quality Promotion Unit (QPU) by the Committee of University Principals (CUP) in 1995. Although established to formulate a quality assurance system for the whole of higher education in South Africa, the reality was that it concentrated its efforts on the universities. Within the universities, the QPU's approach was to concentrate on systems rather than quality itself. Thus, reviews would look at how effective an institution's systems for assuring quality were, in the first place, through examining the mission statement and its objectives. Thus, individual programmes were not examined, rather the institutional self-evaluation was the central way in which an audit was performed. Institutions were not ranked following the audit and, in fact, the actual reports on institutions were confidential to the institution and were not in the public domain.

Within a period of only three years the credibility of the QPU was being questioned and by 1999 it had been closed. There are various reasons for this apparently dramatic move. The Task Team established by the Council on Higher Education (CHE) to evaluate both SERTEC and the QPU (CHE, 2000, pp. 32–3) gives a range of reasons for the failure of the QPU:

> In the first instance, there was little widespread clarity on the purpose and functions of the QPU ... While the QPU expressly set out to assess quality procedures only, there was a clear expectation among the public, and many institutional leaders (including that of the institution concerned) that a report from the QPU signified a judgement on the institution's quality *per se* ... Secondly, ...quality was ill-defined and too relative and that the whole approach was too developmental and lacking a firm judgement ... a more summative approach was needed ... Thirdly ... there was criticism from many quarters relating to both capacity and competence in the QPU, insufficient training of audit panels and inadequacy in the writing of audit reports which all led to a lack of credibility on the part of the QPU. Fourthly ... one of the main reasons for the ultimate failure of the QPU to carry out its work satisfactorily was a lack of resources ... Fifthly, the QPU operated in a context of widespread system transformation.

The somewhat dramatic decision to close the QPU was, in part, a result of the government's determined effort to address all aspects of higher education in South Africa, including quality assurance. It was as a result of widespread consultation that the White Paper on Higher Education (1997) proposed fundamental changes to higher education. This arose partly from the recognition that the move from minority rule to democracy necessarily involved looking seriously at the role of higher education and whether it was fit for purpose. The conclusion, essentially, was that it was not fit for purpose. It was, as indicated above, a very uncoordinated, fragmented, unequal and inefficient system and one that continued to favour the white population. Starting from a position in 1993 where the participation rate for white students was just under 70 per cent and only about 12 per cent for African students there was clearly a long way to go. In fact, although still substantial, the gap between the two participation rates diminished significantly in post-Apartheid South Africa.

The White Paper, as part of its extremely wide brief, addressed the issue of a qualifications framework for higher education. It noted that the former system of separate qualification structures for universities, technikons and colleges, in fact produced barriers between institutions and programmes as well as placing obstacles in the way of widening access. Consequently, a ladder of qualifications has been introduced within a single qualifications framework with appropriate exit qualifications. The introduction of the South African Qualifications Authority (SAQA) was clearly a major step towards achieving a more open and accessible structure.

The White Paper also recognised that the higher education institutions themselves have an important responsibility for quality assurance. However, it also noted that an over-arching national authority for quality promotion and assurance was needed. In this regard a Higher Education Quality Committee (HEQC) was proposed.

The interim HEQC that has subsequently been established is, in fact, a subcommittee of the Council on Higher Education (itself established in 1997 as a statutory body by the Higher Education Act of 1997). The latter has one operational responsibility – to establish and organise a quality assurance system for higher education. The HEQC, arising from the stipulations of the Higher Education Act is charged to:

- promote quality assurance;
- audit the quality assurance mechanisms of higher education institutions; and
- accredit programmes of higher education.

The founding document of the interim HEQC provides useful signposts to the likely future of quality assurance in South Africa. Its starting point was to review the position pertaining internationally and to look at local needs and contexts. The interim HEQC clearly has a major task in hand given the fragmented system it has inherited and to try to arrive at a single quality assurance system that would have validity and confidence right across the higher education system and involving different kinds of provision.

The interim HEQC is committed to introducing a quality assurance system that will be phased in over two years. The kind of system proposed is not too different from those to be found in other countries – a combination of self-evaluation and external validation through peer review in the widest sense. Furthermore, there is a strong commitment to partnership and cooperative agreements with the higher education institutions and with the professional bodies.

References

CHE (Council on Higher Education) (2000), *An Evaluation of SERTEC and the Quality Promotion Unit*, CHE: Pretoria.

Department of Education (1997), *White Paper on Higher Education*, Vol. 382, No, 17944, Department of Education: Pretoria.

List of Contributors

David Dunkerley is Professor of Sociology at the University of Glamorgan, Wales. For many years he has been involved in quality reviews and assessments, having been Vice-Chair of the Social Sciences Committee of the erstwhile Council for National Academic Awards and more recently a member of the Hong Kong Council for Academic Accreditation (HKCAA). He has published numerous refereed journal articles and 14 books, the latest being *The Globalisation Reader* (Routledge, 2000) and *National and Ethnic Identity in Europe* (ULP, 2001). He is currently working on another book for Routledge, *Changing Europe*.

Judith Eaton has been President of the Council for Higher Education Accreditation (CHEA) in the USA since 1997. Before joining CHEA she was Chancellor of the Minnesota State Colleges and Universities. She has served as President of the Council for Aid to Education, Vice-President of the American Council on Education, President of Community College of Philadelphia and President of the Community College of Southern Nevada. She has been a member of the HKCAA since 1998.

María José Lemaitre is presently Secretary General of the National Commission for Programme Accreditation in Chile, having previously held an equivalent position in the Higher Council for Education in Chile. She is the President of the International Network of Quality Assurance Agencies in Higher Education (INQAAHE) and is the representative of the Chilean government at the Working Group for Evaluation and Accreditation of High Education within MERCOSUR. She has published extensively on Chilean and South American higher education matters.

Danie Jacobs originally trained as a physicist but moved into education inspection and policy planning in the 1970s. Since 1989 he has been the Executive Director of the Certification Council for Technikon Education (SERTEC) in South Africa. The Council's role has been to evaluate standards at South African technikons and to award appropriate certificates. His professional interests centre on quality assurance in higher education and especially the methods adopted to ensure quality.

Kwong Lee Dow is Deputy Vice-Chancellor of the University of Melbourne, having previously been Dean of Education. He chairs the Victorian Curriculum Assessment Authority and is a member of the Australian Multicultural Foundation and of the HKCAA since 1992. He is also Chair of the Asia Education Foundation and has been a Council member of the Hong Kong Institute of Education. His reputation as a leading Australian educator has been acknowledged by appointment as Member of the Order of Australia.

John Leong OBE is Chairman of the Hong Kong Council for Academic Accreditation, having joined the Council as Vice-Chairman in 1996. Since then he has spearheaded the assessment work in relation to non-local courses offered in Hong Kong. He has also chaired a number of institutional reviews and presented papers at many international conferences. He is currently Professor and Head of Department of Orthopaedic Surgery at the University of Hong Kong and is President-elect of the Societé Internationale de Chirurgie Orthopédique et de Traumatologie.

Marie-Odile Ottenwaelter is senior consultant in the CIEP, a French organisation for the development of education worldwide. She was formerly employed by the Comité National d'Evaluation (the quality assurance agency for French higher education) where she coordinated over 20 evaluations of institutions and disciplines. She has been involved in various European programmes and has been a consultant in quality assurance related matters in many countries including Argentina, Hungary, Italy, Madagascar and Switzerland. She has been a member of the HKCAA since 1996.

Christian Thune was Dean of the Faculty of Economics, Law and Political Science at the University of Copenhagen until 1989 when he became Chair of the government-appointed Advisory Boards in Higher Education. In 1992 he was appointed Director of the new Centre for Quality Assurance and Evaluation of Higher Education. In 1999 Christian Thune was appointed Executive Director of the new Danish Evaluation Institute that was established by government with the mandate to evaluate all levels and sectors of Danish education. From 1997–99 was a member of the board of directors of INQAAHE and from 2000 has been Chair of the European Network for Quality Assurance. He has been a member of the HKCAA since 1994.

List of Contributors

John Randall was formerly Chief Executive of the Quality Assurance Agency for Higher Education in the United Kingdom. Prior to joining the Agency as its first Chief Executive in 1997, he was Director, Professional Standards and Development at the UK Law Society, with responsibility for professional regulation, education and training of solicitors. He served for five years on the National Council for Vocational Qualifications, and is currently a member of the council of the City and Guilds of London Institute. He is also a member of the Board of the International Network of Quality Assurance Agencies in Higher Education. He has published widely on matters relating to quality assurance in higher education.

Qi Suiyuan is Deputy Director of the library at the Northwestern Polytechnic University, China and has long been an active researcher on higher education management.

Wang Runxiao is the Superintendent of the Institute of Manufacturing Automation Software and Head of the Educational Administration Department at the Northwestern Polytechnic University, China.

Wai Sum Wong has been Executive Director of the Hong Kong Council for Academic Accreditation since 1996. As well as being heavily involved in the accreditation work of degree programmes and of tertiary institutions in Hong Kong she has been instrumental in developing assessment of non-local courses for registration purposes under Hong Long law. She is a founding member of INQAAHE and has taken part in numerous visits, seminars and international conferences worldwide.

Xu Demin trained as a marine engineer and has taught and researched at the Northwestern Polytechnic University, China since 1964. During a period as Vice-President, Dean of the Graduate School, his central concern was the establishment of quality assurance and evaluation systems. He has served as a member of the Academic Accreditation of Academic Degrees Committee of the State Council (PRC) and is presently a member of HKCAA.

Index

Academic accreditation 15, 16–22, 42, 92
Academic Audit Unit 59
Academic Review 6, 57, 62–3, 68
Access courses 61
Accountability 127
Afrikaans 144
Agricultural colleges 147–8
Argentina 116, 120
Ashenden, D. 142
Asiaweek 132
Associate degrees 31
Association of European Rectors 51
Audits 146
Australia 8–9, 123
Australian Medical Council 131
Australian National Training Authority 124
Australian Universities' Quality Agency 8, 124, 137, 141
Australian Vice-Chancellors' Committee 129–31, 135
Authorised Validating Agencies 61

Benchmarking 134
Beynon, J. 2
Bolivia 116, 120
Bologna Declaration 6, 53, 54, 87
Brazil 116, 120
Brennan, J. 4
Bulawayo Polytechnic 148

Campbell, C. 86
Caritus Francis Hsu College 16
Centres of Higher Education 73
Chile 7, 8, 106
China, Peoples' Republic of 5
Chinese University of Hong Kong 11
Cisco 100
Colombia 120
Comitæ National d'Evaluation 48, 50
Commonwealth government 135–6
Consejo Superior de Educación 111–13, 118
Council for Higher Education Accreditation 7, 92, 95, 100, 102

Council on Higher Education, South Africa 152
Council for National Academic Awards 15, 48, 59
Craft, A. 9
Credits transfer 93

Danish Evaluation Centre 48, 50, 76–8
Danish Evaluation Institute (EVA) 7, 70, 78–84
Danish Ministry of Education 72, 74, 75, 88
Dearing, Lord 58, 60
Denmark 6, 7, 70
Distance learning 44, 58, 87, 101–2
Dunkerley, D. 2

Education Commission 29–30
Education reforms, Hong Kong 28
E-education 140
Electronically-delivered education 100–102
European Credit Transfer Scheme 53
European Evaluation Agency 49
European Foundation for Management Development 54
European Network for Quality Assurance 51–2, 87
European quality assurance 47–8
Evaluation method 79–80
Evaluation of higher education, China 40–44
Evaluation studies 3, 41, 46
External audits 136

Federal funds 92
Fordism 138
Franchising 58

Giddens, A. 1
Gilbert, A. 140
Global education 1

Henkel, M. 3
Higher Education Act, USA 100
Higher Education Council, Australia 136

Index

Higher Education Funding Council 60
Higher Education Law, China 34–6
Higher Education Quality Committee 9, 153
Higher Education Quality Council 59, 60
HKCAA 5, 14
Højbjerg, E. 83
Hong Kong 5, 11
Hong Kong Academy for Performing Arts 11, 12, 15
Hong Kong Baptist University 11
Hong Kong University of Science and Technology 11, 54

Indicators 138
Institutional management 66
Institutional quality 66–8, 127, 146
International Association of Management Education 54, 102
International Network of Quality Assurance Agencies 10, 59, 121

Jacobs, D. 9

Knowledge-based society 28, 126
Kristoffersen, D. 71, 83

Learning outcomes 99–100
Learning resources 65
Lee Dow, K. 8
Lemaitre, M. J. 8
Leong, J. 5, 11
Lerotholi Polytechnic 148
Lifelong learning 31
Lingnan University 11, 16
Little, Arthur D. 134

Macleod, D. 142
Marginson, S. 142
Mass participation in higher education 47, 58, 70, 125
McDonaldisation 2, 9
McKinnon, K. 133, 134
Media rankings 132
MERCOSEUR 8, 116–17, 120
Microsoft 100
Milligan, S. 142
Ministerio de Educación, Chile 108, 114

Networked universities 44
New public management 4
Non-local courses 24–8

Open Learning Institute, Hong Kong 21
Open University of Hong Kong 11
Ottenwaelter, M.-O. 6
Overseas qualifications 28

Paraguay 116, 120
Partner institutions 67
Peer review 2, 20, 94
Performance contracts 85
Peru 120
Phare programme 51
Polytechnic of Namibia 148
Professional organisations 92, 126, 131–2
Programme accreditation 113, 130
Private institutions 29, 58, 107, 139

Qualifications Framework 30, 61–2
Quality Assurance Agency, UK 6, 59
Quality Promotion Unit 151–2

Randall, J. 6
Regional accreditors 103–4
Ritzer, G. 2

Schengen Agreement 3
Selectivity 108
Self assessment 80, 81, 85, 96
SERTEC 9, 144–151
Shah, T. 4
Shue Yan College, Hong Kong 13, 16, 29
Socialist higher education 35
Sorbonne Declaration 53
South African Qualifications Authority 150–51, 153
Spybey, T. 1
Starapoli, A. 86
Student fees 58, 71, 109, 126
Student progression 65
Student surveys 128

Teaching and Learning Review 22, 23, 32, 65
Teaching Quality Assurance, China 37–9
Teather, D. 142

Technikons 144–7
Thune, C. 6, 52, 71–2, 78, 86
Transnational Education 54, 55
Treaty of Amsterdam 3

United States Open University 101
University Act, Denmark 75, 85
University of Maryland 101
University of Melbourne 128, 136
University of Paris 53
University of Phoenix 103
Uruguay 116, 120
US accreditation 92–4
USDE 95, 96, 100

Van der Wende, M. 86
Vocational Training Council, Hong Kong 13, 31
Voluntary accreditation 111, 114

Western Governors University 101, 103
Williams, P. 137
Wong, W. S. 5, 11
World Bank 120
World Trade Organisation 55

Xu, D. 5

Zhongxi School 34